Little Victories
A True Story of the Healing Power of Horses

Betty Weibel

Published by Brown Dog Books
Cleveland, Ohio

Copyright ©2019 by Betty Weibel

All rights reserved

ISBN: 9781692591359

Library of Congress Cataloging-in-Publication Data

Notice: The information in this book is true and complete to the best of our knowledge. The author and the publisher disclaim all liability in connection with the use of this book.

This book may be purchased in bulk at special discounts for sales promotions, fund-raising or educational purposes.

For details contact Brown Dog Books,
18955 Fox Road, Chagrin Falls, Ohio 44023 or info@bettyweibel.com.

Manufactured in the United States of America

Cover and interior book design by Yurich Creative

Cover photo credits: Second Story Productions LLC for Fieldstone Farm; The Plain Dealer, ©1995 The Plain Dealer; Lynn Ischay/The Plain Dealer ©2010 The Plain Dealer. All rights reserved. Reprinted with permission. Inside photo credits: Unless otherwise noted, all photos are courtesy of Fieldstone Farm Therapeutic Riding Center.

BROWN DOG BOOKS
Cleveland, Ohio

Dedicated to the hard working staff, volunteers, and horses in therapeutic riding programs around the world and represented in this book.

Written with love and special thanks to my parents, Bob and Nancy.

Preface

Debbie Gadus was living her post-college dream of a career with horses when a riding arena roof collapsed on her during a winter snowstorm. Rescue workers dug her out of the wreckage, doctors saved her life and therapists guided her through rehab and her new life as a paraplegic. *Little Victories: A True Story of the Healing Power of Horses*, shares Debbie's struggles and how horses and therapeutic riding helped her learn to live, and eventually support others with disabilities.

Little Victories takes readers inside the special world of therapeutic horseback riding by telling a second story of the Chagrin Valley Therapeutic Riding Center, which was already in existence years before Debbie's accident. The Center's story begins in a college classroom with an idea, and spans the organization's growth and evolution to become one of nation's top centers, later known as Fieldstone Farm Therapeutic Riding Center.

Following her accident and rehabilitation, Debbie's story intersects with that of the Chagrin Valley Therapeutic Riding Center. Readers go behind the scenes to see Debbie's milestones of learning to ride again, teaching others with disabilities from her wheelchair, running a horse farm and developing a new therapeutic carriage driving program as an alternative for who can't attempt riding.

Little Victories invites readers to take a closer look at therapeutic riding. You will meet some of the horses, volunteers, parents, and students, while seeing the Center through their eyes. The field has grown quickly and likely there is a therapeutic riding center near you due to the evolution of the North American Riding for the Handicapped Association (NARHA), which was later renamed Professional Association of Therapeutic Horsemanship International® (PATH Intl.). Therapeutic riding programs continue to expand, meeting the needs of children and adults, whether they serve a mental or physical disability, contribute emotional support, or handle other challenges that can be met through the unique healing power of the horse. As you read, I hope you will consider volunteering at a local center, make a donation, or tell someone you know who may benefit from learning about therapeutic riding.

Contents

Afterword

Notes and Resources

Prologue

The muffled voices sounded as if they were coming from under water...except she was the one trapped beneath the surface. She felt like she was sinking, along with her horse and the little girl riding alongside her, as the world crashed down on them.

"The world breaks everyone, and afterward many are strong at the broken places."

— Ernest Hemingway

Part 1

Debbie's Story

1

———

A Snowy day

January 17, 1994

The snow began before sunrise. Light flakes floated delicately in slow motion for several hours before turning into whiteout conditions, piling nearly three feet of snow and a layer of ice on rooftops and roads all over the Midwest. Newspapers reported that the National Guard had been mobilized that morning as major highways from Missouri to Pennsylvania were forced to close.

The heart of Ohio's snowbelt – east of Cleveland and inland from Lake Erie – was no stranger to heavy snow and inclement winter weather. Chardon, Ohio, the Geauga County seat, was the snowiest location in the state due to its elevation, impacted when the wind blew across the lake. Kids who were home from school for Martin Luther King Jr. Day took advantage of the opportunity to enjoy some fun in the snow.

The storm didn't keep seven-year-old Emily Glenn from her favorite activity, horseback riding. Although Emily typically rode after school or on weekends, her mother dropped her off at Tannerwood Farm in Chardon that Monday morning so she could slip in an extra riding lesson with Alison "Sunny" Jones, who owned the beautiful farm specializing in Welsh ponies.

Winter pasture time.

When Emily walked into the indoor arena, Tannerwood barn manager Debbie Gadus was already in the saddle exercising a pony named Sunset. The two nodded a quick hello to each other as Debbie rode by and Emily walked her pony, Bouquet, to the corner where the two-step mounting block allowed her to climb into the saddle easily. Emily gave a little sigh of relief knowing she wouldn't have to ride alone, as Bouquet could get nervous without the companionship of another horse.

"Go ahead and pick up a posting trot, Emily," Sunny called after her student had done some warm-up laps. A few minutes later, the ponies were trotting along in the lesson while Emily practiced balancing on the balls of her feet as she stood in the stirrups. For warmth, she and Debbie had decided to ride in their snow suits, instead of traditional riding breeches.

The lesson was winding down just before 11 a.m. as Sunny gave her final instructions to Emily, who followed Debbie along the long wall of the 50- by 100-foot arena. As the riders took their last lap before preparing to pull into the center of the arena and dismount, the wood and metal roof of the indoor riding arena, weighed down by more than two feet of snow, creaked slightly. It was the only warning that the roof had exceeded its weight bearing capacity, but the ponies sensed danger. Sunset, the more skittish of the ponies, bolted as the roof rumbled like thunder, and Debbie pulled back on the reins, startled. "Hey!" Debbie yelled. She thought she must have pulled too hard and knocked the pony over because the next thing she knew, she and Sunset were on the ground.

Debbie blinked several times in confusion as the wood from

the ceiling began crashing down around her. She thought that Sunset was lying on top of her after the fall; she could feel weight on her body. She lay still waiting for him to get up. When the weight didn't move, she realized it was the roof on top of her, not the pony, and that she couldn't move her lower body. Her upper body was mobile, but that didn't help her. She thought she should just take some deep breaths and stay calm as she lay there. With tears stinging her eyes, tasting the sandy grit of arena dirt and dust in her mouth, Debbie wondered what had happened to Emily and Sunny.

2

———

The Accident

January 17 had seemed like an ordinary day, except for the heavy snow that was falling. Debbie started the morning with her usual barn chores, tossing a flake of hay into each stall and scooping pelleted horse feed into the feed bins as hungry ponies stomped impatiently. She paused when she noticed Emily coming into the barn earlier than usual – she had the day off and couldn't wait to ride that morning.

The dramatic roof collapse had spiraled Debbie out of her routine into a nightmare. As she lay buried beneath the pile of roofing materials and snow, Debbie told herself to remain calm as she contemplated the situation. Looking back, she recalled, "I was lying on my side and I remember thinking my knee was bent up a lot higher than it was supposed to go. I was awake the whole time, waiting."

Emily's pony had panicked and bolted, launching her onto the soft arena surface as it ran to safety when the roof caved in. Because she was closer to the door, Sunny was able to get out of the way with the two ponies just as that section of the arena collapsed.

Her heart pounding, Sunny ran to the barn phone and dialed 911. Rescue crews, including paramedics from the Chardon Volunteer Fire Department, were dispatched to the collapsed riding arena. As the first responders walked through the barn door, they were dismayed by what they saw, realizing they had no idea where to start looking for Debbie and Emily.

From her spot beneath the debris, Debbie could hear voices. As a way of coping, she convinced herself that the rescuers would locate her. She felt a little panicked however, when she started coughing up dirt and phlegm and thought, 'Geez, I have internal injuries.' But as she heard the voices getting closer, she focused on helping them find her.

When the rescue workers called out for the girls, they could hear Debbie's responses from under the snow near where they were standing, but they did not hear Emily. However, from her location under the snow, Debbie could hear Emily's cries for help.

"Stay calm, Emily. They are coming for us," she said. But after a little while, Debbie realized she didn't hear Emily any more. She assumed Emily was staying calm and waiting for someone to start digging.

Pinned beneath the roof's wooden support beams, Debbie struggled for enough air to get her voice to work. "I was awake the whole time but I couldn't yell loudly because it was so hard to take deep breaths," she remembered. But she kept crying out as best she could. The sound of her muffled voice continued to aid the rescue workers who were looking for her. They found her about 30 minutes after they arrived. Despite being buried in snow, "I wasn't cold because my snowsuit kept my body warm even after they uncovered me," Debbie said.

Chardon Volunteer Fire Department Lieutenant Larry Gasper was among those trying to locate the girls. "When we found Debbie, she was on her side with her face buried in sawdust. A truss from the roof pinned her foot and there was evidence that another truss hit her in the shoulder," he said.

"There was no warning at all," Sunny told officials when they questioned her about the accident. "When the roof caved, I went down in a ball. By some miracle, nothing hit me." Both ponies, as well as Sunny, had escaped without injury.

Emily's mother, Kim, was on her way back to the farm to pick up Emily with her younger children, five-year-old Henry and two-year-old Martha, when several fire trucks with lights flashing and sirens blaring passed her. She turned to Henry and said, "What an awful day for a fire," because it was so snowy and cold.

As Kim turned her car into the entrance to Tannerwood Farm, not far behind the firetrucks, she faced a nightmare: news that her daughter had been in an accident. Sunny met Kim in the driveway and told her that the fire department was digging through the snow and rubble to find Emily. Kim felt the fear rise through her body and she started to go numb as the reality of the situation registered.

Kim approached the pile of debris that was once a riding arena. She saw dozens of rescue workers and started to cry. She immediately called her husband to tell him the news and said, "I think Emmy's dead."

3

———

The Rescue

Once rescuers located Debbie and lifted the beams off her broken body, she was able to speak more easily and aid in Emily's rescue. As medics worked on her, Debbie reached above her head and pointed to indicate where she last saw Emily, about 25 to 30 feet away. "Over there. I heard her voice from over there," she said softly. In shock, she lay still watching as a snowflake floated slowly above her head and landed on the tip of her dirt-covered nose.

After Debbie pointed to Emily's location, it was another 30 minutes before they found the buried child. "We were yelling 'Emily' the whole time, but she was not hollering back," said Lieutenant Gasper.

Nearly 40 firefighters and volunteers worked together using snow shovels, pickaxes, and their bare hands to remove debris as they searched for Emily and Debbie. The Chardon team was aided by workers from the nearby communities of Munson, Kirtland, and Hambden. "We must have had 25 shovels going at one time," Gasper said. "There was so much snow, so many people with shovels. We had to remove the snow so we could peel the roof away."

Chardon Volunteer Fire Department's Mark Burr told newspaper reporters: "It was quite a process clearing away snow, lifting sheets of corrugated metal, clearing away more snow, lifting more sheets of corrugated metal. We kept coming up on two-by-fours that were lying flat against the sawdust floor, and were thinking, 'Gee there's no clearance. Nowhere for someone to be. No place for Emily.' I thought she was dead. You try your hardest and you keep hoping, but I thought there was no way she could survive that."

Amazingly, prayers were answered and hard work rewarded when Emily was found face-down in the rubble, between two spans of two-by-six trusses. The rim of her riding helmet kept her face far enough out of the sawdust to let her breathe. As Burr uncovered her limp body, he looked for her wrist. "I reached down and checked her pulse first thing. I think in the back of all our minds, we thought she was dead." But when he detected a tiny pulse, everyone breathed a sigh of relief.

While rescue workers were uncovering Emily, another team was working on giving Debbie the medical help she needed. "The snow is coming down too hard and it isn't safe for the life-flight helicopter to operate, Debbie. We are going to transport you by ambulance to Geauga Hospital," one of the EMTs

Barn roof collapse traps two

By Tammy Stables
News-Herald Staff Writer

Firefighters are blaming heavy snow for a collapsed barn roof that buried two Chardon Village residents alive, critically injuring both Monday morning.

Debbie Gadus, 28, of Chardon Village, a barn worker who was on horseback at the time of the incident, was paralyzed from the lower back down Monday after she was

Maribeth Joeright/News-Herald

Firefighters from Chardon, Kirtland and Munson Township – along with neighbors – help clear away snow and metal from the fallen barn roof at Tannerwood Farm in Chardon Township Monday.

told her calmly. Time was passing quickly and after a stop at nearby Geauga Hospital, she felt herself being moved again to a helicopter that would shuttle her to MetroHealth Medical Center in Cleveland, a facility better-equipped to handle major trauma.

Debbie's parents arrived just as rescuers were taking her to the helicopter pad, and she assured them she was okay. In the helicopter she tried not to be sick, which is a body's natural reaction to broken bones. When she arrived at MetroHealth, her condition was listed as critical. Debbie was booked into intensive care with a fractured lower spine.

By the time Emily was finally freed from the debris, the snow had slowed, and she was driven a short distance down the road from the farm to an open area just inside the gates of All Soul's Cemetery. A helicopter had been able to land and was waiting to take her to the pediatric unit of Cleveland's Rainbow Babies and Children's Hospital. When Emily arrived at the hospital, she was listed in critical condition with injuries to her arm and shoulder.

The roof collapse at Tannerwood wasn't the only disaster created by the weather and accumulating snow in Geauga County. Instead of melting before another snowfall, the December snow had stuck. Police received numerous reports of buildings collapsing or being damaged by the combined weight of snow and ice.

"This was the second roof collapse at a barn in a week," said Gasper. "A lot of roofs are not able to handle the heavy snow;

a lot of barns don't have roofs as heavy as a residence," he explained.

Debbie and Emily weren't the only victims of tragedy caused by a collapsed roof that day. In the nearby community of Middlefield, teenagers at an apartment complex had been enjoying the day off at an indoor swimming pool. At 4:30 p.m., most of the kids were climbing out of the pool to head home when there was a loud bang. The flat, snow-laden roof collapsed onto the swimming pool and surrounding deck. Firefighters spent an hour sawing their way through the roof to get to a young teen who was trapped half in and half out of the water between the roof and concrete pool deck. Although the apartment manager was able to pull a six-year-old child from the water, rescuers were unable to save the 14-year-old, whom they found two hours later beneath the collapsed roof.

4

———

At the hospital

Media across Northeast Ohio reported the story: Debra Gadus, 28, a trainer at Tannerwood Farms, was in critical condition with spinal injuries at MetroHealth Medical Center. Hospital spokesperson Terry Pederson told reporters, "She does not have any feeling in her lower body. We don't know yet whether she'll be able to walk or not."

Reports on Emily were a bit more positive: Emily Glenn, 7, was in fair condition in the pediatric intensive care unit at Cleveland's Rainbow Babies and Children's Hospital. Dr. Michael W.L. Gauderer, director of pediatric surgery at Rainbow, said Emily's injuries included a broken arm, three broken ribs, a bruised liver and multiple pelvic fractures. While the injuries didn't require surgery, she would need to leave the hospital in a wheelchair and would not be able to walk again for several weeks while her body healed. If she had not been wearing a riding helmet at the time of the accident, Emily's injuries and prognosis would have been very different.

Emily spoke to reporters from her hospital bed, propped up by pillows with her favorite stuffed animal, "Bunny," under her arm. She looked over at the two photos her family had placed on her hospital bedside table. One frame held an image of her with siblings Henry and Martha. The other was of Emily and Debbie astride their ponies.

While she had been trapped beneath the arena unable to speak or move in the darkness, Emily said she knew she was in trouble but needed to remain calm and think about something else. She told reporters that the first thing that came to her mind was a fairy tale she had learned in school, "The Elves and the Shoemaker," and the second grader started reciting:

"The shoemaker made one pair of shoes, because he only had that much leather. But the elves helped him make the shoes, and they sold for a very high price. And so then he could buy enough leather to make two pair of shoes. And they sold for an even higher price. And so then he could make three pairs of shoes...." And on and on and on the story went through her head while rescue workers above her searched and called and dug.

At one point, Emily said she remembered trying to knock with her fist on the tin roof debris that covered her, and even raised one foot hoping someone would see her. But she was beneath so much snow and material her foot never reached the surface.

"I think I was brave because I did not panic. I knew I had to breathe slowly, because if I breathed quickly I would get tired and fall asleep and they wouldn't be able to hear me. So I buried myself in the sawdust. I wiggled into it because I knew it would keep me warm, and I just kept thinking about the shoemaker," she told newspaper reporters.

"I was up to 105 pairs of shoes by the time they got to me. I heard a man's voice yell, 'We found her!' and then felt a hand touch my wrist," she recalled. "I remember he said to me, 'Emily, you're going to be all right. You're all right.' Then I believed it, too."

Emily's mother was understandably emotional when she responded to media questions. "It's just amazing that Emmy...I don't even want to talk about it," she said. "Mrs. Jones and Debbie were there too and they were all in it together. There is so much love between the three of them."

At Kim's request, Sunny Jones came to visit Emily at the hospital. "Kim told me to come and help with Emily's progress, and I told her I'd be there, because I needed that too. The psychological burden of all this had been really hard," said Sunny. Seeing Sunny reassured Emily that her friend was okay.

Although Emily and Debbie were hospitalized miles apart in different facilities, the two stayed in touch through daily phone calls and compared notes on their recovery. They made up a fun game to measure and compare their recovery based on what food they could eat and when, because they knew that was a medical marker of their progress. "The better you get, the more you eat, so I was the first to eat Jell-O and it was green, and the first to have a Popsicle. It was cherry," Debbie explained of what they called their Jell-O races.

Emily didn't know the full extent of Debbie's injuries, and her only concern was that she get better. Debbie gave her a special message of encouragement: "We're going to ride again Emily."

5
_____

Debbie's outlook

"When I arrived at MetroHealth, they did more tests and X-rays," Debbie said. "It was determined that I needed surgery, but the spinal cord and tissue surrounding it had swelled up, so they would have to wait until the swelling went down before doctors could operate. I learned that they can give you a shot to prevent the swelling, but it needs to be administered within an hour of the accident to be effective. Unfortunately it took them longer than that to dig me out and get me to Geauga Hospital."

She added, "While waiting for the swelling to diminish, they put me in a bed that swings, a hammock-type of thing, and sedated me. I remember my parents arriving at Metro and explaining to them what was going on. I believe I had surgery the next day; however, I don't remember any of that or much of my hospital stay. I just remember waking up in the hospital a day or two later and being very tired. I could not see my back, but the only other injury marks on me were the black and blue ones on my arms from where they had tried to start IVs."

Days after the accident, Debbie learned that her fractured spine resulted in paralysis from the waist down. She told a reporter, "Right now my legs feel like they are asleep. But as far as walking in the future, I don't see why not." Her outlook on walking fluctuated. "Yesterday I said 'Yes'. Today I don't know. I'll probably keep working at it until it happens."

During another newspaper interview she opened up and reflected, "If this had happened a year ago to me, I would have committed suicide. But I've been working on my self-esteem this last year. I was trying to change my outlook on life. I was really starting to feel good about myself, my career, my life. I was seeing someone. Everything was clicking for me. Then this happened. I had never been a very religious person, but since the accident, I find myself praying more."

Debbie had started to develop a relationship with an old high school friend before the accident, and even considered moving out of Ohio to live closer to him. However, as they talked by phone from her hospital bed and she shared the details of her accident and rehab, he admitted he didn't think he could handle the situation. Their budding relationship broke off. She told a friend with a smile from her bed, "Well, I guess this means I have to start all over again."

Debbie took her recovery one day at a time and remained positive, vowing to her many supporters that she would either ride or drive horses again. "I'm doing OK. Thumbs up. I'm doing all right."

"There are no guarantees, although I'm told that my spinal cord wasn't severed and so there's a chance I might walk again. Everything right now is geared to prepare me for the worst. There's no sense of waiting to see if I will be able to walk again. I need to be able to take care of myself. I'm lifting weights and doing push-ups to build my upper body strength. The last two mornings, I dressed myself. The idea is to be able to live on my own again eventually," she said, and she had hope that would happen.

As Debbie lay exhausted in her hospital bed with all the monitors and medicine dispensers cluttered around her bed, she drifted in and out of restless sleep. She remembered how her day had started January 17, feeding the impatient ponies their hay and pellets. It was the last day she would walk down the barn aisle on her own. That routine ended forever when the roof caved in on her.

6

———

Looking to the past...Growing up and the college years

As a child, Debbie Gadus' love of animals intensified when her father, John, took her to a local stable. Many people don't like the smell the first time they walk into a barn. But from the very beginning "the smell of the tack and horses brought me a comfortable feeling," she recalled.

During her sophomore year in high school at Eastlake North, she joined the riding club. Debbie gained experience and took riding lessons throughout high school. She worked cleaning stalls in exchange for her lessons, which she thought was a fair trade. By the time she was 16, she started sharing her passion for riding with others as a summer instructor at a popular local camp, Chincapin.

"I taught English-style riding in the same place that I learned to ride, at Chincapin. I continued off and on after school, on Saturdays and during the summers, teaching girls aged six to 12 who were beginners and just learning how to jump small fences. I enjoyed teaching, seeing the spark of 'I get it' once in a while," she explained.

Founded in 1957 by Alison "Sunny" Jones, Camp Chincapin was part of the Red Oak family of camps. The camp focused on the fundamentals of English riding with a strong emphasis on safety and horsemanship. Dependable lesson horses and passionate, experienced instructors created a fun learning environment for all levels of riders. "It was a year-round commitment managing the horses and barn and directing the summer camp as well as spring and fall riding programs," Sunny said of the operation.

Debbie knew early on that she felt a connection with four-legged creatures great and small, whether it was dogs, cats, cows, or horses. When she considered what to do after high school, she didn't think twice. She knew she wanted a future with animals. "I was serious about my studies in high school because I thought I wanted to go to school to be a veterinarian and I needed to have good grades. I worked for Hough Catering and saved my money for college," she said.

Debbie wasn't a girl who stood out in a crowd, nor did she like to call attention to herself. She was more comfortable in the barn than attending social events. She stood 5-4, was of medium build and wore thick glasses. People might describe her hair as dirty blond with a little strawberry, and although it would get lighter in the summer, she never colored it. She didn't like makeup unless it was a special occasion.

She seldom smiled and spoke softly when she was unsure of herself. Even the clothes she wore helped her blend in—her preference was nothing bright or too stylish.

When Debbie considered her college choices, she didn't look at many options. Having grown up in Ohio, it seemed natural to look within the state's border, so she chose Findlay College.

In the 1980s, it was a growing school in rural Northwest Ohio. The small, friendly campus in a lovely town had a culture of accessible instructors and staff, which was an ideal environment for Debbie, who warmed up slowly in new places. The animal science programs offered different specialties leading to work in the animal and livestock industry. Debbie was immediately attracted to the pre-veterinary medicine track that prepared students to enter veterinary school, which required an additional three years of education after the four-year undergraduate college degree.

During her freshman and sophomore years, Debbie worked in the cafeteria and the library to supplement her college funds. However, after her freshman year, she decided that the pre-vet program wasn't right for her due to its heavy academic challenges, so she changed her major to animal biological science and management. That general animal science degree offered broader learning experience with most farm species, including beef and dairy cattle, swine, sheep, goats, llamas and horses. That path of study prepared students for handling and managing animals, owning or operating a livestock facility, and working in the small or large animal agriculture industry.

Aside from the academic studies that led to a four-year bachelor's degree, Findlay students could participate in numerous student organizations, including special interest clubs and sports, such as Western and English horseback riding. Debbie was vice president, and later president, of the pre-vet club even though she had decided not to pursue that area of concentration. However, her new major shared some of the same classes and activities, which made it a smooth transfer.

Debbie gained experience running Findlay's barn

operations, and in her junior year she became the assistant student manager of the pre-vet barn, which housed all of the non-equine animals. She advanced to student barn manager her senior year and graduated in 1987.

7

Going to work and finding meaning

Debbie had dreamed of moving west after college graduation. More than anything else, she wanted to work with cattle or sheep on a ranch. But she lacked experience working with such livestock and couldn't find a job in that area. She did, however, have experience working with horses.

Finding employment in the horse world wasn't difficult, and after she returned to her home in Northeast Ohio, she took a job at a farm that raised Standardbred horses for harness racing. In addition to cleaning stalls and mowing pastures, she cared for mares and foals. When the work slowed in the winter, she supplemented her income by teaching and cleaning stalls at other horse facilities that needed help, including Twin Pines and Lake Erie College. Much of the work was low-skilled and low pay. None of it was what she envisioned when she graduated with a degree from Findlay College.

"I was trying to sort my life out. I wanted to find a way to break free and cut the cord from the life I was living. I needed to figure out how to support myself without being on horse-person wages," she said of life after college.

Then, two years after graduating, Debbie started to work at Tannerwood Farm in Chardon. Although it was still employment in the horse world, she had some decision-making responsibility, and the job provided an important plus: she could live in a rental apartment not far from the farm. Other than being away at college and living on-site in a shared house while she worked at Lake Erie College, Debbie hadn't lived in her own place until she started working at Tannerwood. Having her own space gave a much-needed boost to her pride and confidence.

Tannerwood Farm. *Courtesy of Sunny Jones.*

Since the early 1960s, Tannerwood Farm had been the family home of Sunny and Ted Jones, a couple Debbie knew from their Camp Chincapin. It was also in the early 1960s that the Jones family fell in love with Welsh ponies. They bought their first mare in foal from a breeder in New Jersey and soon thereafter bought a stallion from the prestigious Liseter Hall Farm in Pennsylvania. They purchased several more fine ponies, including their first carriage driving team of ponies, from Jean DuPont, the owner of Liseter Hall. Over the years, the Jones family purchased top stock from other breeders in Canada and New York and eventually established their own line of registered Welsh ponies. They bred, trained, and sold ponies for competition, pleasure riding and carriage driving.

While most things usually are measured in terms of inches or feet, in equine terms a unit of measurement is a "hand," which is equal to four inches. Ponies stand no taller than 58 inches (14.2 hands) at the top of their shoulder or withers. Any pony taller than that is considered a horse by most American standards. There are numerous breeds of ponies such as the Welsh.

At the peak of its operation, Tannerwood had 40 ponies, including four stallions. "We had seven foals in one year and a full teaching program that included Camp Chincapin. It's been a very happy and rewarding journey," Sunny said.

Trees and flowers lined the driveway to Tannerwood Farm and a gate to the drive was opened during the day for farm operations. Visitors would pass a guest house and another white building that housed offices before reaching the first L-shaped barn where the stallions, a few riding horses and ponies lived, along with a miniature donkey.

The big barn on the property lay a little further along the drive with more stalls, a tack room and wash rack. The driveway came to a circle and the indoor riding arena was to the right near the paddocks where horses could graze and play while they were turned out.

The riding arena wasn't very large, but being under a roof, it was ideal for lessons and exercising the horses and ponies, especially when the weather was inclement. There was a small enclosed viewing area where guests could watch lessons.

Beyond the barn operations, the drive continued north past a big pasture to the residence, then to more fields and pastures. Parallel to the drive, a separate driving and carriage trail led to a fenced riding field, and beyond that, there were many acres of woods. Jumps were sometimes set up in the field adjacent to a large driving dressage arena. Trail riding has been an important part of the equestrian experience, along with carriage driving through the woods, up and down hills, across streams and even through a water crossing at one of the two ponds on the property. All of this provided diverse training for riders and carriage drivers. Tannerwood Farm was a horseman's paradise.

Debbie worked at Tannerwood for several years and eventually became the equine manager. She was responsible for daily feeding and care of the horses and ponies. When she entered the barn each morning and turned on the lights she loved to hear the soft nickering from some of the horses as they greeted her. Others hurried to stand up from a nap, as they squinted in the light. A few of the ponies would whinny, saying, "hurry up, I'm hungry."

Debbie cleaned stalls, exercised ponies and gave them basic training under saddle and in harness (for carriage driving), handled the young foals, and scheduled their appointments with the farrier (blacksmith) for shoeing and trimming feet; the equine dentist and the veterinarian. She assisted with the overall operations, including occasionally teaching riding lessons. Although there was variety every day, the basic routine varied little, since horses are comfortable with routine. When there is a change in feeding time, for example, horses get impatient and nervous, and some may pace or kick the walls of their stalls, which can lead to an injury.

A typical Tannerwood day started just after sunrise for Debbie, who lived in an apartment over a garage just down the road from the farm. She would feed the horses and ponies, first dropping a flake of green leafy hay from the overhead loft into each 10 x 10-foot stall. Then she went down the aisle and scooped grain from the large feed bin into individual feed tubs in each horse or pony's stall. Some of the animals needed special vitamins or supplements, and she made sure they were distributed in the proper dosage to the right horse. As they were munching hay or chewing the last of their grain, Debbie walked down the aisle checking each automatic water dispenser, stopping at the front of some stalls to dip her hand into the waterer and pull out lumps of wet hay the ponies had left behind while dunking their breakfast.

After breakfast, Debbie would get started with pasture turn-out. The horses and ponies that weren't going to be ridden that morning were led out to pasture in small groups. The mares went in a large fenced pasture near the barn. Another pasture was allotted to the geldings, castrated male ponies. A third pasture was reserved for the pony stallion. Friskier than all the others, he was turned out alone to insure he wouldn't kick or nip at the mares and geldings.

As soon as the horses were outside, Debbie would get to work cleaning each stall, a job she found relaxing because of the systematic approach that gave her time to think about her day. During the process, Debbie moved the leftover uneaten hay to the corner of the stall. Using a thin-tined pitchfork, she removed the larger piles of manure and put them in the wheelbarrow, gently shaking the loose dry bedding out of the pitchfork and back into the stall so she didn't waste clean shavings. The stall's bedding, spread across the floor, consisted of soft pine wood shavings delivered from the local lumber mill. After that, she moved around the outer edge of the stall in a circular direction, sifting through the sawdust to remove wet spots left from urine. Certain horses were always messy, and she dreaded doing some of those stalls. One in particular would sometimes leave manure in the water bucket, which meant Debbie to empty and scrub it. Other equines kept neat stalls, only messing in the corner. Their habits were so distinctive that Debbie could tell which horse lived in a stall without looking at the brass nameplate on the door.

Around 10 a.m., Sunny Jones usually would come down to the barn from the house and help turn out the horses and ponies. She and Debbie would ride those on the exercise schedule for the day. Riding lessons with students were usually on the weekends or after school, but some ponies needed extra exercise.

Debbie would break from her chores at mid-day and serve the ponies their lunch, a small portion of grain for some and a flake of hay for everyone.

After lunch, Debbie's job included housekeeping tasks such as cleaning the tack − saddles, bridles, and girths. She would refill the grain bins in the feed room, clean cobwebs from the corners, groom ponies that had not been ridden, and perhaps work another pony. Dinner time was around 3 p.m., so she would repeat the process, bring the remaining ponies in from pasture, sweep up, and leave by 3:30. She did this daily with a half day off on Wednesday and every other weekend off.

Although the work was very repetitive, Debbie did enjoy working with Sunny, often riding during the lessons Sunny taught. This gave Debbie a chance to exercise the ponies with another rider and work on their manners getting along with others.

Debbie's days were busy, leaving her tired and ready for bed each evening. She had little time for anything else in her life, although Sunny didn't hesitate to try to get her involved in projects outside work.

"I remember one day Sunny asked me about volunteering at the Therapeutic Riding Center. I never thought of working with horses in that environment. I didn't think I could handle the riders with disabilities. I am just not a huggy person who likes dealing with emotional tragedy, so I had no interest," Debbie said. She was content with her life as it was, and focused on her job and living on her own. Little did she know how much her life would change, and with it, her views of disability and therapeutic riding.

8

———

Back to reality and rehab

In February, about a month after the accident, people expected Debbie's optimism to wane. But she remained determined and positive, wearing her white sneakers as she lay in the hospital bed, motionless except for rolling her head, eyes and hand movements. She grinned when anyone asked about her shoes. "You get dressed, you put on your shoes. It helps me believe I am going to walk again," she said, looking toward her feet. However, her prognosis weeks after she remained at MetroHealth Medical Center was not as positive as her outlook.

As she reflected on her time in the hospital and in rehab, Debbie explained, "I slept a lot, and my room was in one of the hospital towers. That is a good location to be if you need a lot of help because the nurses are in the center of the circle and close when you call. As I recovered though, it was not such a good location because I could hear every buzzer when it went off. I was starting to have trouble sleeping because of the noise and was going to ask for sleeping pills, but that was when I learned I would be moving soon to go into the rehabilitation phase of my recovery."

The transfer to rehabilitation, or "rehab" for short, was simple because it was just shifting from the MetroHealth Center to its Center for Rehabilitation. "It was located in another building nearby, so it was just a matter of moving my bed from one room to another. My first morning after moving to rehab, Drs. Frederick Frost and Graham Creasey visited me. They told me, 'The good news is you can still have children. The bad news is you will never walk again.' But as far as the good news, children were never in my plan," said Debbie.

"Dr. Creasey went on to tell me, 'Here in rehab, you will learn to do things from the wheelchair.' He would be my rehab doctor for many years. My surgeon, Dr. Wilbur, came to visit at some point over the next few days and told me not to believe them. 'You will walk again,' he told me," she said. There were many conflicting reports for Debbie to consider because even the doctors didn't agree on her future.

As part of her recovery process, Debbie kept a journal, taking notes on the process, observations, and her feelings along the way. She worked with a psychologist while she was in rehab so that her mental outlook could support her physical healing.

Writing in her journal, she made many notes:

"While in the hospital, they made a mold of my upper body. I can't remember the technical name for it, but I called it my turtle shell. It was two plastic pieces that Velcro together, to stabilize my upper body while my head, arms and legs stuck out. I wore it over my clothes almost all the time. I was also told I could not sleep on my stomach, which was a problem because, of course, that is how I was used to falling asleep.

"So with my turtle shell on, I began physical therapy and occupational therapy. At first in physical therapy we worked on muscle strengthening and balance. I learned to transfer from the bed to the chair and how to use a sliding board for transfers that were longer. After a while, there came a point where they were not sure what to do with me as I was not like many of their female patients. Most of the time women entered rehab with weak upper body strength, so their rehab focused a great deal of time building that up. But after working with horses and doing barn chores, I already had good upper body strength. It didn't take long before I learned to maneuver the wheelchair, pop up curbs, and transfer from the floor to the chair, just in case I was to fall out.

"As luck would have it, my physical therapist, Holly Hamilton, was a horse person, too, and had her own horse. We got along great and were friends for many years after my rehab. We even stayed in touch for a while after she moved away from the area.

"Occupational therapy was where I learned to do things from the chair, like make the bed and cook. The rehab facility had an area called Easy Street. It was set up so patients would practice moving through a store and getting things down from shelves with a reacher, bouncing up curbs if there were no ramps available to use, and opening doors and moving through them. I also practiced carrying food trays, and dealing with public places like banks, because they have high counters.

"I had two different roommates during my six-week stay in rehab, but most of the time I roomed with Nancy, a woman who had been hit by a truck. She had many issues to deal with and we got along. She was the person who told me I could refuse treatments, which I had never considered. Every day, they would give me heparin shots because I was not as active as I once was and with broken bones they are concerned with blood clots forming. These shots are given into a fatty area, which was in my belly. This is where my loss of sensation begins so the nerves there are hypersensitive and the shots really hurt. I asked the nurse if I could get the shots anywhere else, and she gave me one in my thigh. My whole leg swelled up, and it was still swollen when I was discharged a month later. It was after that incident that I began to refuse the shots.

"Eventually, Nancy had to transfer to a skilled nursing facility to heal more because she wasn't fully ready for the next phase of rehab. She had a colostomy bag and refused to take a supplement to make it not smell so much, which was a problem for me at times. I was having my own troubles with my bowel routine and was often sick to my stomach. Each day when they changed her colostomy bag, I would start throwing up again. Eventually I learned how to manage my bladder and bowel.

"A typical day during my rehab stay was: breakfast, wash up, get dressed, go to physical therapy, lunch, occupational therapy, dinner, television, and my bowel routine was done at night. They did offer some activities such as art therapy, but I had my cross-stitch needlework, so I did not participate.

"One morning we were running late for physical therapy

and it was during the time I was dressing myself. Because we were late, the nurse was helping me dress and she tied my shoe. I stopped her and asked her to retie it because she had put the bow in the middle of the shoe, but at that point my bows were off to the side of the shoe, and you know the therapist would notice, right? There was a lot of hurry up and wait, because you did not go to therapy or tests by yourself. You needed to wait for someone from transport to take you everywhere.

"I remember one patient, a young man who had broken his back. He had fallen off a ladder painting houses to earn money for college. He was finishing up rehab, but wasn't sure where to go next because his family did not want anything to do with him and his disability. I just cannot imagine what that had to be like for him.

"During my stay, I received many phone calls and visits from family and friends and got many cards, even some from people I did not know. I don't know why I received so much publicity, but because of it I got many letters and cards and flowers, from friends and strangers. An entire sixth grade class taught by a former teacher of mine sent me cards. I heard from people from my elementary school who I hadn't talked to since I was in school. It was just awesome and I really appreciated their mail and their prayers.

"My visitors included family, of course, immediate and extended. Father Gillas from St. Mary's Church came to visit, which really surprised me as I had just joined the church after being away for a long while. Sunny's priest came to visit several times as well. Friends from Twin Pines Stables visited one time and I remember that because they brought me food from McDonald's. It was a fish sandwich, which I loved and tasted so good because it wasn't hospital food," she wrote in her journal.

Debbie celebrated an emotional birthday at MetroHealth on February 22, and her parents surprised her by getting permission to bring her oldest cat, Smidget, for a visit. The little black and white cat behaved well and cuddled with Debbie. "I appreciated it so much. They brought her in a carrier and we closed the room door, but she never left the bed. I guess they got some strange looks in the halls and elevator."

Debbie's journal continued, "During another Saturday visit, a friend from college drove all the way from Columbus with her husband to visit me. It was a day I was not feeling so well. Her husband started saying that he knew I would walk again...I'm not sure if he meant in this life or the next, but I had accepted the fact that I would not walk again. So I said something back to him, to the effect that I did not need this sh** right now. I lost a friend that day.

"It was a couple of weeks into rehab when it hit me that I really wasn't going to walk again. I remember getting out of bed to wash up and rolling up to the sink to brush my teeth. I reached up to get the toothpaste and could not reach it so I went to stand up...but I couldn't. I cried as I tried, but not too much, because my father and brother happened to be there at the time. I still cry when I think about that time. The only other time it bothered me was at mass, because at church I couldn't use the kneelers. I don't know why, but for the rest of rehab, my attitude was JUST GET ON WITH LIFE, do what I can. Get back on a horse, she wrote in her journal.

"The big test before going home was going out to dinner in The Flats entertainment district of Cleveland. My therapists, another patient, and I took a van to get to the restaurant. It was much easier for me to go out to dinner than the other patient. He had a higher level injury and had a difficult time feeding himself his spaghetti dinner because he did not have full use of his hands." By the time she left the hospital, Debbie realized she was better off than some of the others she had met.

While Debbie was in the hospital and rehab, Sunny

monitored her progress and care to be sure she had the best doctors available, even exploring electrode options at a Veterans Hospital. Debbie said, "I was fine with my outcome but when the doctors confirmed there was nothing anyone could do for me, Sunny took it very hard and cried."

She wrote in her journal: "My recovery, and the prognosis that came with it, was harder on Sunny and my family than it was on me. Sunny wouldn't give up and wanted me to go to her doctor after I was home, which I did. He reviewed my case and said, 'Looks like you are doing well. What can I help you with?' I asked him to help me tell Sunny that I was good, and there was nothing else to be done. He did, but she still hurts."

Sunny was going through her own issues at that time and was gradually losing her hearing. Debbie was glad that she had started learning sign language before the accident. Although Sunny had received implants to aid her hearing, it was helpful that the two friends could use sign language when needed. It was another special connection that bound them even closer.

9

———

Moving back home

March 1994

It was St. Patrick's Day when Debbie finally left MetroHealth rehab and moved back into her parents' home. The doctors' predictions had been correct, and the spinal cord injury was complete as a result of fractures to her two vertebrae, T11 and T12. Rods were inserted into her back, and she had no feeling from her waist down.

The greatest emotional challenge Debbie now faced was losing her independence after being used to living on her own, only to return to her childhood home. This tough period of living at home stretched into years. "I was never one of those people who could fall backward and trust people to catch me, but after my accident I had to trust people, because I needed help at times," she said.

Returning home was as unfamiliar as moving into a strange place because her new life was very different from anything she knew before the accident. Now Debbie maneuvered with a wheelchair. The four cats she had at her former rental home had been displaced as well. Two of her cats lived with a cousin and two others were at her parents' home. But the move was a necessity for Debbie because she wasn't ready to live alone.

The Gadus family home. *Courtesy of Debbie Gadus.*

The Gadus' home was a simple three-bedroom, one-bathroom ranch in Eastlake, on the far outskirts of the eastern Cleveland suburbs. The location made it convenient for Debbie to continue outpatient therapy and get to appointments that were closer to home.

"It seemed like there were thousands of doctor appointments as I was trying to get my life on track again. My parents were living in a house with my brother and sister. I took over the living room until they could put on an addition to give us more room," said Debbie.

"My morning routine took two hours, and trying to get out of the house was a challenge—I was always late. We had one bathroom for five people." The Gadus family later added another bedroom, a bathroom and a dining area.

"While I was recuperating, I occasionally wore braces to help me stand, and it was a lot of work. They were called reciprocating gait orthosis, and they locked my hips and knees so I could ambulate, a medical term for 'move.' It involved moving the walker forward, then shifting my weight to one side so I could swing, scissor-fashion, forward, then shift the weight the other way and swing the other leg forward to move with the walker. I did it off and on – more because it helped me bear weight on my legs so the bone density would be maintained, than to actually get from point A to point B. I stopped this process when my shoulder started bothering me, as I was still using my upper body a lot," she explained.

"My personality is to be a fighter. I like to give people a hard time," she said. "I understood they were worried and wanted to help – I was Daddy's little girl, and Mom drove me around for two years. Even though she was allergic, she would still take me out to the barn."

She added, "I think my family is okay with my loss now. Dad has learned not to help unless asked, which got him in trouble at an assisted living facility where my uncle was staying. When an elderly woman yelled at him, saying, 'Can't you see I need help?' and he replied to her, 'My daughter tells me to wait until asked.'"

When Debbie was growing up, her family life was very traditional, with stay-at-home mom, Rose, and dad, John, who worked at Hough Bakery his entire career. Debbie was the oldest of three children, followed by Melinda, three years her junior, and Alan, who was five years younger. The kids got along like most siblings, with minor squabbles. They had a strong sense of family, like many whose ancestors immigrated to the United States. Rose's roots were German/Slovenian, while John's family was Polish/Slovak.

The sisters shared a bedroom, Alan had his own room, and their parents slept in a bedroom that was converted from a one-car garage. When the parents moved into the house in 1964, it was more than 20 years old and Eastlake was considered remote. But in recent years, the highway changed the landscape and the population grew because commuting to Cleveland became faster and easier. All of the houses on the street had a similar look, and only the homeowners would notice the subtle personal touches that made them their own.

As a child, Debbie participated in many activities, some influenced by family and some by peers. "I took a set of art lessons, tennis, played a season of softball; I was in Girl Scouts from Brownie up to Cadets from second through ninth grade. One of my grandmas taught me embroidery, which I still do. The other taught me to crochet, which I do very little. My uncle started me on collecting stamps, which I still do. I took some guitar lessons as a young teen and in college but could not play now if I had to."

Although she loved animals, Debbie didn't grow up with many pets other than a Siamese cat named Duchess that had been a wedding present for her parents. The cat became very attached to Debbie. But after Duchess died, the Gadus family remained pet-free because Rose had developed allergies that made her very ill.

Debbie's accident had a major impact on her family, and the move home changed the way everyone lived. They became a focus of attention not only in the media, but also with concerned friends and the community. They were uncomfortable being in the public eye that focused on them after the accident.

Debbie's brother, Alan, didn't share his thoughts easily and was at his parents' house when the accident happened. When Debbie was helicoptered to MetroHealth, he said, "the media wanted our family to make a statement, but we did not. No one in the family has ever talked to the media. Debbie is the only family member to ever talk to the media about the accident when they visited her in the hospital. We keep our problems to ourselves and do not ask others for help. We prefer to solve any issues in private," he explained.

Alan understood Debbie well. "Debbie was an independent person. She believed if a man could do it, she could do it better. She did not need anyone's help. For example, when she is in her wheelchair, you do not push her. If she gets stuck you wait for her to ask for help."

After the accident, "Debbie was forced to allow other people to help her and she no longer could be independent," said Alan of his sister's difficult transition. As far as Debbie's goals of returning to her life with horses, Alan said, "Debbie loves horses. It is funny to see people afraid of horses because they are bigger than a person, but Debbie was never afraid of horses, even in her wheelchair."

Horses were always on Debbie's mind as she recovered. The goal of working with horses again gave Debbie all the hope and determination she needed for the new challenges she faced.

"Start by doing what's necessary, then do what's possible and suddenly you are doing the impossible."

— Francis of Assisi

Part 2

A Therapeutic Riding Center's Roots

10

___

The Classroom incubator

1977 Lake Erie College, Painesville, Ohio

It was the first week of a new semester at Lake Erie College in 1977, and the upper lobby of the school's George M. Humphrey Equestrian Center was hosting its "Teaching Riding for the Handicapped" course. Located in the northeast corner of Ohio, Lake Erie was a premier women's college with one of the finest equestrian programs in the country. The school had recently expanded to offer nonresidential options for male and female students through its partner, Garfield Senior College, which shared the campus.

At the front of the classroom, the professor looked over the rim of her glasses as she pointed to the chart on the whiteboard. She ran down the list of physical, emotional, cognitive and social benefits in each category, hammering each word in staccato style. Gretchen Singleton's petite size contrasted with her voice, and it boomed over the students seated in front of her.

Gretchen Singleton. *Courtesy of Lake Erie College*

"Improved balance, mobility, muscle tone, coordination, and posture; enhanced independence, increased concentration, and self-esteem. Therapeutic riding is proven to be highly motivational and enriching, as you will see when our students set aside their crutches, wheelchairs, and disabilities and settle into the saddle later during the riding/teaching portion of this course," she announced.

Started with a few horses in a small shed behind the college campus, the Lake Erie College equestrian facility became a reality in 1971 with the construction of the George M. Humphrey Equestrian Center. Named for a local horseman who was a former U.S. secretary of the Treasury, the center was just a few miles from the college campus. The college added a unique equestrian studies major to educate women in that field and promote careers in teaching riding, training horses, and running an equine facility.

One of the many reasons for the growing success of Lake Erie College's Equestrian Studies program was Gretchen Singleton. She poured her positive energy into teaching, whether it was her dressage riding lessons, an early morning foxhunting class with the nearby Chagrin Valley Hunt, or Teaching Riding for the Handicapped, which introduced Lake Erie College students to teaching people with disabilities.

Gretchen grew up in West Virginia with a love for all animals, especially horses, and a gift for inspiring others. Early in her career, she trained at the Cheff Therapeutic Riding Center in Augusta, Michigan, which was one of the first equestrian facilities built especially for the purpose of serving children and adults with special needs in North America.

Gretchen's experience at the Cheff Center was applied to her

Riding for the Handicapped class at Lake Erie. The college class was very popular, often filling before the course registration deadline each year. The course curriculum combined classroom lectures with weekly practical experience assisting while Gretchen taught her community therapeutic riding lessons to local youth with disabilities.

The Cheff Therapeutic Riding Center conducts a certification class.
Courtesy of Cheff Center.

In preparation for the Riding for the Handicapped lessons scheduled for later in the week, Gretchen used the classroom time to review the benefits of therapeutic riding. As she spoke, a few of the students' eyes traveled from the front of the room to the glass viewing window that overlooked the riding arena, where horses were being exercised. However one student stayed focused on Gretchen's every word.

It was hard to miss the focused young man who seemed out of place at a women's college. The other students assumed he must be a Garfield Senior College student, or someone from the community who had elected to audit the course. He looked older than everyone else, and his hair was dark and thinning, but his eyes were fixed on Gretchen, absorbing every word of her lecture.

Kevin Ellison was the most engaged student in the Riding for the Handicapped class and asked questions that showed a high level of interest and knowledge of the topic. He also volunteered answers when he got the chance, which was a bit annoying to the other students. Throughout the multi-month course he never missed a class, and his enthusiasm for the subject rivaled Gretchen's. He elected to enroll to satisfy his own curiosity, rather than for college credit.

When he looked back on his time at the college, Kevin recalled, "It was the spring of 1978, and I already had a college degree from the University of Notre Dame. I grew up with a love of horses and was taking riding lessons with a local professional and teaching a little on my own. Many of the kids I was teaching didn't want to be there; it was their parents who wanted them to be riding, and it was frustrating. I had started auditing some of the classes at Lake Erie College, like the Equine Lameness course taught by veterinarians from Randall Equine Clinic. Then I decided to take Gretchen's Riding for the Handicapped class. I loved Gretchen, and the students in her lessons wanted to be there...so did the volunteers," Kevin recalled.

Following the classroom session, the students in the Riding for the Handicapped class reassembled at the entrance to the riding arena. They awaited the arrival of the mini-bus that transported the students with disabilities from the Bessie Benner Metzenbaum Center, operated under the Geauga County Board of Developmental Disabilities.

The Lake Erie students listened to Gretchen's instruction. "Alright everyone, listen up for your assignments," she said and formed groups of three. "You will be a team assigned to Drummond. Go ahead to the barn and get him tacked up," she said to three seniors standing toward the back of the group. Kevin and two other seniors were assigned to tack up Linus, then the rest of the class got their assignments. Everyone was nervous, anticipating a chance to put into action all they had been learning in the classroom.

As the three senior girls walked slowly out of the indoor riding arena to the attached stables toward Drummond's stall, they grumbled to one another. "I have so much homework to catch up on today." Their minds were not focused on the duties in front of them, as Gretchen's voice pierced the cold air again. "Remember, Drummond needs a fleece girth on his saddle since he has a rub. Hopefully he won't be too cranky today," Gretchen shouted after the girls.

Quieter now, one girl led Drummond out of his stall while the other two brushed off the stall dust and saddled the small roan horse. The girl walking Drummond has been assigned as the horse's leader for the lesson, while the other two would be the side-walkers, who made sure their student didn't slip off balance and fall sideways from the horse. They didn't know yet who their student would be, but they knew they would circle the arena during the lesson as part of the rider's team to provide assistance if needed.

As they led the horse down the aisle to the arena they heard a shriek, "That's him. Here comes Drummond now!" A teen who didn't look much younger than the college girls was pointing one curled hand while the other clung to a metal walker that framed her body. Amy had trouble containing her excitement in anticipation of her riding lesson. As the trio neared her, Amy reached her trembling hand forward and Drummond raised his nose to accept her gentle pat. Then the team moved the horse to the side to align with a wooden ramp that led to a platform level with the saddled horse, so Amy could get on easily.

Amy turned her walker slowly. Her body moved jerkily, not in the straightest line. Her head swayed a little to the side and she adjusted her eyes forward as others assisted her up the ramp to the mounting platform, where the volunteers would help her into the saddle.

Gretchen reminded them, "Amy needs to do a crest mount." This meant that she would sit down on the saddle sideways from the mounting platform which was level with Drummond's back. Her team of assistants positioned themselves, one directly in front of Drummond making sure he was standing balanced and close to the mounting platform, and the other two stood on the sides to make sure Amy was balanced, and to position her legs correctly as she swung them over Drummond's neck before sliding them down as far as they would go.

Once she was ready, Amy was handed the reins and with one volunteer at Drummond's head, the other two on each side with a hand on Amy's thighs to balance her, they moved away from the mounting area. It was the moment for which Amy had waited for all week, and in a loud stutter she said, "Walk on!" as they went into the arena.

Gretchen stood in the center, surrounded by a pair of upright poles with a small cone on top of each one that was stacked with soft rings, as well as a pair of poles on the ground and two orange cones about 50 feet apart. "Good afternoon, Amy, how are you today," Gretchen asked. Amy's team stopped by Gretchen so she could check that the tack was adjusted correctly as Amy replied, "Great, now that I'm here."

"Would you please walk your horse around the arena, stopping Drummond at the letters A, B, C and E, and count to five after each letter before moving on to the next. Then ask him to walk on again. We will put your feet in the stirrups after that," Gretchen instructed as the team moved forward to follow her directions with the other riders in the class. After reversing direction and repeating the exercise, Amy and her team made their way back to Gretchen and parked in the center of the ring. The warm-up exercise helped Amy's legs relax and lengthen, so she could put her feet into the stirrups. As the team adjusted the stirrups to the correct length, Gretchen rechecked the tack and made sure Amy was sitting as tall and centered as possible.

Gretchen began the lesson and spoke gently but firmly, instructing the three riders as well as the college students who made up the support teams. "When you get to the poles with the cones, stop your horse, drop your reins, and try to reach with your right hand to take the ring off the left pole and place it on the cone on the right pole. Side-walkers, you may need to lean the pole toward the riders a bit, but make sure they are reaching and keeping their core centered. Crossing the midline from the center of the horse is almost always beneficial to our riders. When you are done, pick up your reins and walk around the arena again."

After each team did this exercise in both directions, Gretchen instructed, "When you walk on, proceed to the two poles on the ground, and when you reach the first one, pick up your two-point position and hold it until you have crossed over the second pole. Remember to lean slightly forward, grab some of the horse's mane partway up the neck, and stand slightly in your stirrups so your rump is off the saddle and stretch your heels down. This exercise will help your balance and strengthen your muscles."

Gretchen continued her instruction and encouragement for each rider. "Amy, try to keep your eyes up so you can see where you are going. I love where your hands are. That's it, Amy! Your head is balanced so much better when you keep your eyes looking forward." And to the student leader she boomed, "Sarah don't get ahead of Drummond, stay at his throatlatch. The horse can't use himself properly if you are dragging him along."

After the riders repeated the exercise, Gretchen instructed them to sit back in the saddle, and as they approached the first cone, they could pick up a trot to the second cone. "As you prepare for the trot, sit up nice and tall, stretch your heels down, and shorten your reins. Ask your horse to trot with your voice and a slight squeeze with your legs. When you get to the second cone, ask your horse to walk with your voice and pull back on the reins and release when he comes to a walk." Amy squealed with delight because trotting was one of her favorite parts of riding. She could not help herself as she giggled continuously from one cone to the next and then reversed and repeated the exercise. The college student volunteers looked from the horse to the rider and watched carefully while they performed as a team. It was easy to forget this was the same girl who moved along the ground so slowly and unsteadily with the aid of a walker.

"What a fantastic lesson, everyone. Let's do a cool-down lap so our horses can relax before they go back to their stalls. Then we will line up in the middle of the ring for the dismounts. Amy, would you please line up closest to the gate?" Amy did as Gretchen instructed, happy not to have to walk any further than necessary through the arena footing with her walker.

"For the dismount, Amy is able to do a croup dismount because the lesson has relaxed her muscles enough, but be aware that each student is different, and some will do a crest dismount," said Gretchen. She explained that Amy should drop her reins and stirrups, move the left stirrup in front of the saddle so she doesn't get caught on it, and lean forward while a volunteer helped bring her right leg back and over the croup (behind the rump) of the horse before being helped off Drummond to the ground and her walker.

"Class, be sure to thank your horses with a rub on the neck and say thank you to each of your volunteers, and I will see you next week," smiled Gretchen. "Leaders and side-walkers, after you put the horses and equipment away, meet me in the classroom and we will discuss what went well and what areas we could improve on for next week."

Before she moved away from Drummond, Amy stopped close

to his shoulder and put her arms around the neck of the little roan horse. His ears pricked forward and he arched his neck as he put his muzzle close to the girl. From a distance, it looked as if he were hugging her back. Amy smiled and whispered to the horse before letting go and returning her grip on the metal walker. She moved slowly and shakily back toward the waiting bus.

11

———

The Chagrin Valley Therapeutic Riding Center takes off

After Gretchen Singleton's Teaching Riding for the Handicapped class concluded for the school year, Kevin Ellison didn't take any other Lake Erie College classes. He did, however, visit the Cheff Center in Michigan to explore therapeutic riding further, and his inspiration soon grew into action. Kevin started his own weekly therapeutic riding program using borrowed horses and volunteers. Later, after it was well under way, Gretchen saw an article about Kevin's program in the local newspaper and was very pleased that her course had ignited a flame in one of her students. She wasn't surprised that it was Kevin Ellison.

Kevin started the Chagrin Valley Therapeutic Riding Center, Inc. (CVTRC) in 1978 in Russell, Ohio, with eight students with special needs from the Metzenbaum Center. They rode once a week on borrowed horses with the help of a handful of volunteers who traveled to a local farm, Del Ray, owned by a local businessman and polo player.

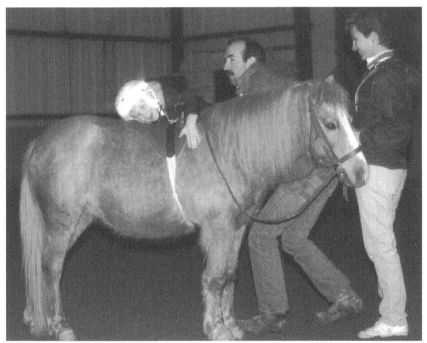

Kevin Ellison assists a young student.

Horses selected for the trial program lessons included Mushroom from Shaker Heights Day Camp, Alex from the Chagrin Valley Hunt Club, and Twistin' from dressage trainer Charlotte Bailey. Several local farriers donated services to make sure the horses' feet were trimmed and shod. Saddles, bridles, and other tack were loaned, and later donated, by Schneider

Saddlery, a local retailer and horse equipment manufacturer.

The borrowed horses were selected for their special ability to conduct themselves with the composure needed to be a partner for the rider, not to be the focal point of the lesson. They had quiet temperaments and didn't object if their riders sat off-balance, moved awkwardly or approached with crutches. These horses were also accepting of the volunteers who needed to hold the riders in place while acting as side-walkers or leaders who guided the horse.

The trial was a success, and private students soon joined the program. The following year, the CVTRC program began holding lessons at the hunter/jumper stable, Dorchester Farms, which was owned by Roland (Rollie) and Harriet Kraus in Kirtland. In addition to boarding horses and training fine hunters and jumpers, Rollie was a newspaper columnist for *The Plain Dealer*, Ohio's largest daily newspaper. He reported on the area's bustling equestrian industry, as well as national equine news, including horse racing and horse shows.

The lessons at Dorchester ran all day on Mondays with school groups attending from the Metzenbaum Center and the Julie Billiart School, which served students with unique learning and social needs. Private therapeutic riding lessons were held on Monday evenings in the indoor arena, and the loaned horses were transported to the barn via horse trailers with volunteer drivers.

Sometimes lessons tested a rider's skill through gymnastic exercises, such as placing a ring on a cone. The riders often missed and repeated the exercise multiple times, but in the process, they gained skill and confidence. In addition to riding, ground lessons taught students horse care without being in the saddle and were an important part of the therapeutic riding experience. Physical and occupational therapists helped define the skills on which the riders needed to focus and set goals for their lessons.

Kevin's enthusiasm about the Chagrin Valley Therapeutic Riding Program promoted awareness of the program, as did articles Rollie Kraus wrote in the newspaper, and support continued to grow. In 1982, the Ride-a-Thon fundraiser was a creative take-off from the walk-a-thons used by other charitable groups, utilizing horseback riders instead of runners. Participating trail riders solicited community donations for every mile they rode. Eventually, the idea caught on, becoming an annual event raising money for therapeutic riding.

For years, Kevin's Chagrin Valley Therapeutic Riding

Center continued holding lessons at multiple locations, including Kevin's own backyard. Volunteers were kept very busy transporting horses and equipment via horse trailers and trucks, and the number of students and volunteers, as well as community support, continued to grow.

Kevin tested holding satellite programs at various locations around Northeast Ohio that were convenient for the groups of students: Edwin Shaw Hospital in Akron, Heather Hill in Munson, Our Lady of the Wayside in Avon, and the Sunbeam School in Cleveland. If there wasn't a facility or suitable location available, the lessons were sometimes held in a parking lot, but safety was always the top priority.

As the Chagrin Valley Therapeutic Riding Center program attracted more students from across Northeast Ohio and traveled outside its Chagrin Valley territory, Kevin decided to change the name and dropped the words "Chagrin Valley." The new name was simply Therapeutic Riding Center, or TRC, for short.

12

———

Chagrin Valley Therapeutic Riding Center
continues to grow

The growth of TRC caught the attention of KC Henry, an experienced therapeutic riding instructor who studied at the Cheff Center after she graduated from college. She had taught in multiple locations, having moved nine times in 10 years for her husband's job before coming to Ohio. She took her work very seriously and was ready to focus on her career, for which she had studied and worked hard to pursue. When she met with Kevin Ellison to talk about teaching at TRC in 1985, she thought she was interviewing for a paying job.

As they discussed the position, Kevin's suggestion that she volunteer her time because it was a non-profit organization with limited funds was not received favorably by KC. After much discussion, they finally agreed that KC would be paid for the hours she taught lessons, and would assist as a volunteer in raising funds so TRC would have money to pay her.

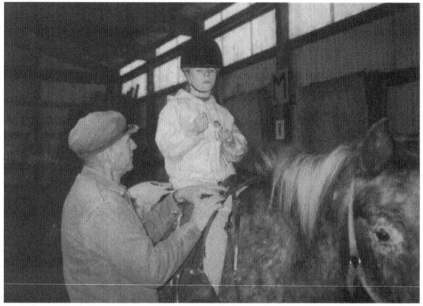

Dick Hambleton talks with a student during a lesson.

KC applied her skills and knowledge from other therapeutic programs and began building a more structured program. Among the volunteers she recruited for riding lessons was Dick Hambleton, a rider himself since he was 18. Dick noticed an ad in the newspaper and learned that TRC was looking for help with the program. He was retired from his business career when he signed up to volunteer at Dorchester Farm, not far from his home.

Dick had a gift for coaxing the most out of his students and making them feel comfortable. He earned their trust and got even the youngest students to open up. Dick volunteered with one young girl who was afraid to hold the reins and control the horse. After working with her for a while, she finally took hold of the reins, but still refused to pull on them to stop the horse.

Dick volunteered regularly for her lesson, walking alongside the child on some days and leading the horse on others, depending on his assigned job. On the last day of the riding series, the girl finally gained the courage to pull back on the reins to halt the horse by herself. Dick never forgot when he heard her soft voice whisper under her breath to herself, "I did it." It was just one example of the rewarding little victories that would keep him returning to volunteer for more than 30 years, even after he reached age 90. "So many things I see as a volunteer may not seem like much, but they really are," he explained.

Not far from Dorchester Farms, the Lake Metropark System had taken over operation of Locust Farm, which included a stable and a heated indoor riding arena. The property was integrated into the park system's unique Lake FarmPark, which was home to many farm animals and attractions, including horseback riding. Kevin worked to build a relationship with the FarmPark so he could use their spacious facility for his lessons, and in 1988 TRC moved its program there. The organization still shipped the horses by trailer, along with equipment and volunteers, to their new site on lesson days. Therapeutic Riding Center held its first Special Olympics equestrian competition at the FarmPark the following year, with 22 students participating.

With the move, the overall number of students in the program grew to 119. However, when the FarmPark eventually opened its doors to the public on a daily basis, new issues arose. The increased public attendance and foot traffic presented safety issues and distracted the special needs students from focusing on their riding. It was not an acceptable trade-off for the facility, and once again, Kevin and KC were in search of a venue that would better suit their needs.

Kevin and KC decided to make a big change, and instead of searching for another loaned facility, they made the commitment to get their own space. They leased five stalls at Salmor Stables on Bell Road in Newbury. This meant the horses did not need to be transported back and forth and could live at Salmor, where lessons were held four days a week. The move resulted in additional growth, enabling the organization to serve 125 students.

During its moves and expansion, TRC was fortunate that dedicated volunteers such as Dick Hambleton continued to travel to the new locations to donate their time. Leasing the stalls at Salmor led to TRC's biggest growth period, although there were still many challenges.

KC remembered, "The riding program was extremely rudimentary at Salmor. It was an old facility that flooded, and the water froze when a pipe broke in the winter. There was no indoor bathroom either, and the office was in one of the horse stalls because there was so little space." However, the team worked around the problems to serve the students.

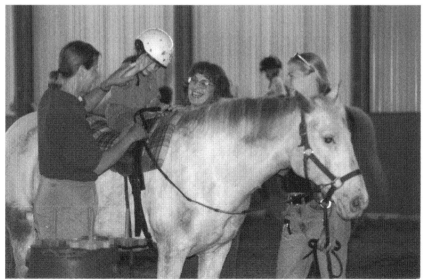

Physical therapist Bobbin Davis (left) helps a student hold the reins.

One day, Dick was volunteering in a lesson with a little boy who was more fascinated by a tractor parked in the corner of the riding arena than the horse he was riding. Due to the lack of storage space, there was no place to store the tractor, so it was blocked off by orange barrels, but clearly visible, making it a distraction to some students and a challenge for the instructors. As the lesson wrapped up and the boy was taking a final ride around the arena with his leader and side-walkers, the child make a bold move to leap from the back of his horse onto the tractor. Dick moved faster and caught him in mid-air. The following week the volunteers covered the tractor with a tarp so it was no longer visible during the lessons.

As the benefits of therapeutic riding became better known, TRC wasn't the only small program in the area. Susan Lloyd, a hunter/jumper trainer, founded Western Reserve Riding for the Handicapped in 1979. Susan offered lessons for the disabled at her own riding stable, where she also gave hunt seat lessons and put on horse shows for able-bodied riders. It was during one of Susan's horse shows that KC met Bobbin Davis, a physical therapist who worked with Susan's program. KC got to know Bobbin, and she began working with TRC's program as well.

Bobbin suggested games for the students with appropriate goals for each individual. She emphasized posture and movement while in the saddle, and her contributions made an immediate impact on the program. It continued to evolve and improve with time through the contributions of many talented people.

The TRC program was run like a business, with close attention to costs. Based on TRC's expenses, which included leasing stalls and caring for horses, the actual cost of a riding lesson was calculated at $37.50. However, Kevin and KC knew that not all students could afford that. They suggested a fee of $10 per lesson, and most parents were happy to pay that share for their child to ride. The rest of the cost was covered by donated funds that they raised from special events.

The program continued to grow, as did KC and Kevin's responsibilities and their workload. Eventually, Kevin leased the remainder of Salmor Stables so they could offer riding lessons six days a week, and they made the decision to hire more help and added a full-time head riding instructor. Lynnette Klessig (later Stuart) knew about TRC through her friend, TRC supporter Carol Horner Donaldson. They rode together at the Chagrin Valley Hunt Club and Carol's family hosted a TRC fundraiser, Hay Day, at their Spring Hollow Farm. Lynnette decided to interview for the riding instructor job at TRC.

"I had a college degree in public relations and journalism and was doing freelance marketing projects. Carol suggested I attend the TRC Annual Meeting to learn more about the program and possibly consider volunteering. When KC told me at the meeting that they were looking for a head riding instructor, she invited me to come out and ride for her. I got on without a hard hat to ride and was stopped. 'No, no, safety is important' KC told me," recalled Lynnette.

"I got the job in the end and was told it was full-time and low pay. There wasn't really any formal training. Dick Hambleton was the first volunteer I worked with and he suggested we set up some cones," she said of her teaching introduction. "The barn was rundown – we called it rustic and tried to make it as nice as possible. We had a tack room that had a lot of mold growing in it – that was our volunteer area – and we had a tiny room for offices," Lynnette said, reminiscing about what she encountered when she arrived at her new job.

13

———

National attention and affiliation

The Lake Erie College Riding for the Handicapped class and its program continued serving students until 1983, around the time Gretchen left the college to pursue new opportunities. Some of the students, as well as riders, who participated in that program later joined the Therapeutic Riding Center and other area therapeutic riding programs. Around the country, the benefits of therapeutic horsemanship were sparking the growth of new programs and riding centers, while the industry was already well- established in Europe.

The popularity of therapeutic horseback riding worldwide took off after Lis Hartel, an award-winning dressage rider from Denmark, gained attention in Europe. Despite being impaired by polio, Hartel took the silver medal in Dressage at the 1952 Olympics in Helsinki. Medical and equine professionals in

Europe began to implement programs for riding as a form of physical therapy. Word of these developments spread to the United States and Canada, and therapeutic riding centers began opening in North America as well.

Two of the first professional therapeutic riding centers were the Community Association of Riding for the Disabled, founded by J.J. Bauer and Dr. R.E. Renaud, in Toronto, Ontario, and the Cheff Therapeutic Riding Center, founded with the help of Lida McCowan in Augusta, Michigan.

A group of passionate individuals recognized the need to start an organization to act as an umbrella association and provide information and resources on therapeutic riding. In 1969, they met and established the North American Riding for the Handicapped Association (NARHA). The goal was to promote safe and effective therapeutic horseback riding throughout the United States and Canada. Membership in NARHA grew to include centers ranging from small one-person programs to large operations with multiple instructors and therapists.

In addition to the resources it offered, NARHA provided formal training and certification for instructors, sanctioned riding facilities and set standards for therapeutic riding. The organization created an annual awards program to recognize and encourage those who were doing the best in the field on a regional basis, as well as nationally.

The tiny backyard Therapeutic Riding Center that began with eight students grew to a successful program that gained NARHA attention. As the operation grew, TRC became more structured and added a board of directors. The volunteer board consisted of business and community leaders who gave valuable advice to TRC and developed a five-year plan for the future, so they were no longer making decisions on a short-term basis. Part of that long-range plan was for TRC to build its own facility, which also drew admiration from its peers in the growing field.

Kevin knew that TRC was in good hands and on a strong path for the future when he made the decision in 1986 to leave his executive director position to pursue his personal business interests. He remained on the TRC Board of Directors, but passed leadership on to KC, who would serve as executive director for the next 14 years.

Therapeutic Riding Center gained NARHA recognition and awards for many of its accomplishments, and Kevin was honored to be named NARHA Regional Volunteer of the Year in 1991. The following year, TRC's therapy horse, an Appaloosa named P.C. (Perfect Chance), was named National Therapy Horse of the Year. KC also earned NARHA recognition and was named NARHA's National Director of the Year. The awards continued in later years as TRC gained attention and admiration.

*"All the world is full of suffering.
It is also full of overcoming."*

— Helen Keller

Part 3

Debbie and Therapeutic Riding Center Come Together

14

_____

Back in the saddle

November 1994

After the accident, Debbie had moved back home and was adjusting to living with her parents, as well as to being permanently paralyzed from the waist down. The Gadus family built an addition to their Eastlake house so Debbie could have her own room and move around easily in her wheelchair. She had learned to drive a car with hand controls and was also learning to take small steps with the aid of braces and a walker.

During her recovery process, she sent a personal message of hope to Emily: "We're going to ride again." Debbie's mother, Rose, summed up her daughter's progress: "She's done a lot more than her medical team expected. She's constantly on the go. She's picking up the pieces and going back to her life."

When no one was around and she was left to her own

thoughts, Debbie couldn't help but feel resentment about the accident. That was particularly true when she had to ask for help or when she encountered people who thought she needed help, even if she didn't. While it was a freak accident, she couldn't help wondering, 'Why me?' However, after some time passed, there was a new question. She found herself asking, 'Where do I go from here?'

After all the therapy she had been through, she knew her best remedy would be to get back in the saddle. Ten months after promising Emily that they would ride again, the day came for Debbie to attempt regaining an important part of her life.

During her recovery, the social and health care workers had tried to discourage Debbie from working with horses because of the physical demands and risks involved. They were concerned that she would be disappointed with her loss of ability, so they tried to steer her toward other activities. However, "the doctors knew how important it was for me to ride again and that horses were my life. I felt there was no life for me outside of horses with my background and training, and I didn't want a future sitting in an office. I wasn't willing to throw that part of my life away and give up," said Debbie.

She had to do a lot of begging with her doctors. "And even

then, I had to twist their arms. Every time I went in for an appointment I asked, 'Can I ride yet?'" she said.

Chagrin Valley Therapeutic Riding Center staff
and volunteers at Salmor Stables.

Sunny Jones first told Debbie about the Therapeutic Riding Center operating at Salmor Stables. In fact, it was Sunny who once suggested that she volunteer there, and she was still a close friend and cheerleader for Debbie. Although Debbie never wanted to work in an office, she accepted a volunteer clerical position at TRC, where she wrote grant applications and sometimes supported fundraising efforts.

About a month later, she was admitted to TRC's riding

program as a student. "Since Sunny had been working at TRC as a volunteer already, I think she got me into the program," Debbie said.

In preparation for Debbie's first ride, her family had to make some special accommodations, including adding mountain tires to her wheelchair so she could move through the indoor arena's deep footing.

Lynnette Stuart was Debbie's instructor for that first lesson. "When Debbie finally came out to ride, we had two people lift her up onto the horse—one person on each side of her. After she was secure in the saddle, side-walkers flanked each side of the horse the entire time she moved around the ring, while another person walked in front of the horse, leading it slowly," said Lynnette.

The horse selected for the first ride was Star. The mare was a small Morgan who had been donated to the program. "She was cute, very smooth-strided and short, which made it easy to reach up and work with Debbie," said Lynette. At 125 pounds, Debbie was quite light, unlike some of the heavier male students.

Several people were on hand to assist for Debbie's first ride, including volunteer Dick Hambleton. When he led Star out to the arena, the team didn't know what to expect. They all knew about the accident because it had been in the news.

Although it was only a 10-minute lesson, getting on a horse was a defining moment in Debbie's life, and it gave her a feel for riding again. Her legs hung loosely like a rag doll, and it was a very different riding experience than what she was used to, but she was back in the saddle.

THE PLAIN DEALER

OHIO'S LARGEST NEWSPAPER $1.25   *****   CLEVELAND, SUNDAY, JANUARY 22, 1995

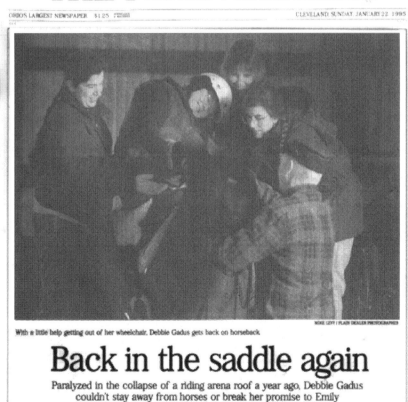

With a little help getting out of her wheelchair, Debbie Gadus gets back on horseback.

MIKE LEVY / PLAIN DEALER PHOTOGRAPHER

Back in the saddle again

Paralyzed in the collapse of a riding arena roof a year ago, Debbie Gadus
couldn't stay away from horses or break her promise to Emily

Front page news January 22, 1995. *The Plain Dealer © 1995 The Plain Dealer.*
All rights reserved. Reprinted with permission.

Lynnette remembered, "We had lots of difficulty with Debbie's legs. I had never worked with a person with paraplegia, so it was trial and error. I remember she was very nervous and not trusting. She had lost sensation in her legs and seat, and having been a rider before, it was disorienting for her. She couldn't feel her seat bones move. As she rode down the long side of the arena and came to a turn, she said 'whoa, whoa' but it was more to herself than her horse because it felt so odd to her."

It was challenging for the team to figure out the best way to work with Debbie as her legs moved about and wouldn't remain in the proper position. "She had no control of her feet and they would fly in and out of the Devonshire stirrups, which are enclosed in leather so the foot can't go through and get lodged in the stirrup. I thought about what to do and got the idea of rubber bands because they could be attached to the stirrup leathers and to the girth to keep her leg in the right place, but for safety it was okay, too, because they could break if needed," Lynnette explained.

The first lesson was brief "so it was a positive experience, and we wanted to get Debbie on and off as quickly as possible that first time. After she got started, we let the lessons go longer, but it is very tiring for the rider," said Lynnette. Debbie was exhilarated and exhausted—her atrophied muscles, combined with the tension of her nerves, added to her exhaustion. "After the first lesson was over, I could see a half -smile from Debbie behind a face hidden by thick glasses," added Lynnette.

15

———

Life goes on for Emily

January 1995

The one-year anniversary of the tragic accident was just another day for Emily. Physically, she was back to normal activities, sports and riding. Mentally, she seemed completely recovered without so much as a nightmare. But she was uncomfortable talking about the accident and all the attention it brought her, and about being called "brave" and "courageous." She really just wanted to forget that the whole thing had happened and move on with her life. She returned to riding at Tannerwood Farm but admitted to being nervous when thinking about riding in indoor arenas anywhere. However, a year after the accident, the indoor arena at the farm had not been rebuilt and there were no plans to do so.

Emily's mother, Kim, told a reporter her daughter showed

no lingering signs of the accident. "As an adult, it's easy to read a lot into it. We talk about the accident. We look at pictures. We get together with Debbie and Mrs. Jones [Sunny]. You pick up the pieces and move forward." But her mom did see subtle changes in Emily that no one else would notice. "She's been where none of us have been, and she's come out of that with a sense of grace and strength. It's a real quiet strength."

Her younger siblings were impacted by the accident as well. Henry was still uncomfortable visiting Tannerwood Farm. Months later, her younger sister, Martha, was still speaking about the day "Emmy had the accident."

After the accident, Emily had received an outpouring of cards, letters and gifts from friends and strangers. But the best gift came from her father, Jim, who offered her a choice of any present. Emily requested a puppy, and they scoured newspaper ads for days before visiting a farm to pick out a black Labrador puppy she named Jackie.

After all they had been through, Emily and Debbie remained friends, and despite their age difference, that friendship didn't change. Emily visited Debbie at home and when she was riding. "We would always ride together and play with ponies and have races before the accident. We used to have fun and talk a lot.

She is still the same old Debbie," Emily said.

On the one-year anniversary of the accident, Sunny Jones stopped by Debbie's home to visit and brought her a violet. She wanted to tell Debbie how proud she was of her amazing progress. The next day Sunny paid a surprise visit to the TRC to watch Debbie ride. Sunny knew the benefits of therapeutic riding from her own volunteer experience and had been determined to get Debbie involved at TRC. During many of the lessons she attended, Sunny would watch silently from the sidelines in a small office where Debbie couldn't see her.

After the roof collapse and long road back to the saddle, Sunny reflected, "Our life plans changed and thanks to some amazing inner strengths and positive attitudes which Debbie developed, we connected more personally and meaningfully through the Therapeutic Riding Center. Debbie was, to the amazement of all — even her doctors — back on a horse." It was just the beginning, however, as the two friends would continue to work together for the benefit of TRC.

16

———

Taking more risks

After finally getting back in the saddle, Debbie continued returning to the Therapeutic Riding Center for weekly lessons on Wednesdays. She worked up to 30 minutes of ride time, and eventually an hour, making adaptations to improve her experience. For example, a blow up pillow to sit on made her more comfortable, as she was prone to sores.

Instructor Teresa Morris, who met Debbie while assisting with her first lesson, was impressed with Debbie's determination. Although Debbie was relatively newly "healed" and it was somewhat risky to start riding again, Teresa saw her determination and resolve. She knew that Debbie's goal was to ride her own pony, Spanky, again and be independent.

"Spanky was a large grey pony I purchased from a local

trainer with the intention of reschooling and selling him. I rode him a few days a week (before the accident) and kept him at another barn where I was helping a lady train some Arabian horses," Debbie explained.

"Debbie never met a challenge she didn't accept," Teresa said. "When she first started riding again after the accident, she was way more willing to take risks than I, her instructor, was. She was the first to suggest riding with two dressage whips on either side in lieu of her legs that couldn't propel the horse forward."

Riders signal the horse to move forward by applying pressure from both legs. Without the use of her legs, Debbie needed to find another way to communicate. "Previously, I had been encouraging her to exaggerate her upper body movement to cue her horse to move forward, but she thought that that was too incorrect for an accomplished equestrian. We tried her idea, and she was right. A light tap with a whip behind her leg kept her body still and resulted in more stability, which in turn made her feel safer and more confident," explained Teresa.

During her lessons, Debbie wore chaps and a riding helmet as she practiced a series of exercises, not unlike the ones she had used in the past when she was teaching new riders balance

and confidence on horseback. For example, arms outstretched to the side or hands on the hips while stretching tall in the saddle all help the rider. To practice coordination while riding with another person, Debbie interacted by using a plastic baton holding a plastic donut and trying to transfer her donut to the other person's baton as she passed.

In the winter, however, Debbie took a break from lessons at Salmor because it was an emotional time for her. "That first winter, riding again was difficult. Although the accident wasn't in the forefront of my mind, my body would always react when the snow was sliding off the roof," she said of the times she needed to ride in an enclosed arena.

Dick Hambleton was usually the volunteer on duty for Debbie's lessons. "Debbie also had a lot of difficulty continuing on a regular basis because she was battling pressure sores that resulted in her having to return to the hospital," he remembered. In spite of all the issues, Debbie didn't give up. "Debbie was anxious and uncomfortable, and we tried a different pad on the saddle so she would feel better. Today we have a special saddle pad for new riders that helps us determine pressure points where riders can get sore, but back then, it didn't exist," Dick said.

After Debbie had been riding again for several months, the team at TRC had an opportunity to demonstrate therapeutic riding during a Lake FarmPark public event, HorseFest. The only problem was that they didn't have a mobile mounting ramp for Debbie to use once they arrived for the exhibition. Teresa suggested pushing Debbie's wheelchair onto the bed of her truck from a hillside, but the idea was quickly discarded by those concerned for safety and the unprofessional appearance of that approach.

One thing Debbie hated about using a wheelchair from day one was that well-intentioned people had the urge to lift her up curbs and steps in her chair; it made her feel very vulnerable and insecure. But Debbie wanted to do the demo so badly that she was willing to let the TRC team help her get to the top of the FarmPark's four-stair mounting block any way they could.

A mounting block is a solid three-foot square structure that allows the rider to get on the horse from a position level with the saddle. One side of the block has small steps to climb to the top, but while helping Debbie, the team would bypass the steps. "The stairs were just an illusion because none of them was bigger than a footstep. Instead, she let us lift her up onto the 36-inch high block and from there she could get onto the

horse," Teresa said. "Our demo was awesome."

Typically, someone who uses a wheelchair needs total assistance to get on a horse. Because Debbie was driven by her personal goal of independence so she could ride her own horse again, she had to think of a way to be able to get on Spanky with the least amount of help. She developed her own technique of getting onto the horse's back. After much trial and ungraceful error, and with the help of Star, the very patient therapy horse, Debbie developed a method to transfer herself with so much finesse that observers would often miss it. She could slide seamlessly from her chair to her horse in one easy motion.

As Debbie's confidence in the saddle grew, so did her desire to increase her independence. She had moved Spanky to the TRC barn so she could ride more often. She wanted to take him out for a trail ride at the public Cleveland Metroparks Polo Field in nearby Moreland Hills. It was a big step to ride in an uncontrolled environment where anything could happen. Debbie and Teresa made plans with another TRC instructor to drive a trailer down to the polo field. They enlisted the help of Teresa's son to walk with them and help Debbie get aboard her horse. "Again, we did not have an easy solution for mounting, but Debbie agreed and helped us devise a way to fireman-carry her from the chair up onto a mounting block and then onto her pony. It wasn't graceful or dignified, but it got the job done. Spanky was as steady as they come," said Teresa.

"We were all up and ready to have a great day on the trail. Debbie had been training for this ride. We weren't going to stay out long, but a ride on the trail is much more challenging than a few laps around the arena, and more fun. Debbie was getting (tired) to the point where we were thinking about turning around to head back when Spanky stopped suddenly in mid-stride just as he was about to land a hoof on a snake sunning on the trail. We had just been walking, but nonetheless, Debbie was unseated and fell off. Our worst-case scenario unfolded right there: Debbie on the ground in the middle of the park and, without any feeling below her waist, no idea of whether or not she was hurt. Since she had landed mainly on her upper body and everything below looked straight, she decided to get back on and ride home," added Teresa.

"This time getting Debbie into the saddle was even more difficult, but there was no one around to see the pushing and pulling while Spanky stood like a soldier. Anyway, we headed home, mission accomplished, and the snake slithered away unscathed," Teresa said.

Debbie later took Spanky in the Ride-a-Thon, the group trail ride at the Cleveland Metroparks facility, where riders solicit donation pledges for every mile completed to raise funds for TRC. In her spare time, she worked on teaching Spanky to pull a carriage. Eventually, she made the decision to sell Spanky, because she didn't have enough time for riding and caring for her own horse. Debbie felt it was a good move for everyone, and Spanky went to a good home with a family and all the attention he deserved.

After she was in the saddle again, Debbie didn't want to stop and continued to ride regularly at TRC. "It's the only thing I've done since the accident that felt like it did before," she said. She told one newspaper reporter who was following her progress, "I have no idea how far I can go. Every time I mention jumping, people look at me like I'm nuts," she said with a smile.

17

———

Working at Therapeutic Riding Center

Debbie had started volunteering at TRC in the fall just to see how much she could do. After riding in lessons for a while, she was the one who brought up the idea of teaching to the head instructor, Lynnette.

"I knew I couldn't go back to work at Sunny's place now, but I didn't know what I could do. While I was riding at TRC, I got to know Teresa, who was the barn manager and responsible for the Equine Management Team (EMT)," she said. That friendship led to Debbie teaching new volunteers and directing the EMT, a group of volunteers she trained in the finer points of horse care.

The EMTs were important to TRC. They were responsible for testing the horses that arrived for potential donation to the program. They also kept the horses neat and tidy with extra care beyond the pre-ride grooming. They held them for the blacksmith, trimmed manes and whiskers, unloaded hay, exercised horses when needed, kept track of feed, and more. There were eight volunteer EMTs when Debbie started working with them, helping expand their knowledge by teaching them about horse psychology, nutrition, tack-fitting, and health maintenance.

Volunteers were key to TRC, and the growing program was a well-oiled machine, recruiting, training and retraining assistants with new education classes. Beyond the EMTs, some of the other important volunteer jobs for experienced horsemen included training horses, providing extra care and turning them out to pasture. Those who worked in the riding lessons with students were given specific assignments, such as the lead volunteers who made sure the horses were ready for lessons and managed other volunteers, oversaw mounting and assisted instructors, as well as leaders who were in front of the horse. The side-walkers spotted the rider during lessons. Other jobs included office help and data entry, while vocational education aides were involved as well.

Debbie knew all of the volunteers by name and grew comfortable in the small facility. She began speaking up and gained confidence in her new job. She was looking for more hours of paid work to supplement her income when she took on the full responsibilities of barn manager.

The job included ordering hay and sawdust, as well as overseeing the care of the horses. TRC wanted someone dedicated to doing the job on a part-time basis, and Debbie's prior experience made her a perfect candidate.

"As barn manager, one of my responsibilities was to see that the horses were looking their best for upcoming student horse shows. This meant we would clip the long whiskers on each horse's muzzle, some of the longer hair under the jaw, in their ears, and on their legs, and trim their bridle paths at the top of their head. The fastest and easiest way to do this is with electric clippers, and most horses are fine with this. However, we had one horse that thought the clippers were going to eat her alive. To help her relax a little I gave her a sedative," Debbie said. The mare was so tall that she needed to elevate her power wheelchair high enough to reach the horse's ears and top of her head, but even with the sedative, the mare refused to cooperate. She raised her head high and moved back and forth to avoid the clippers.

"I had a small group of volunteers helping me, and much to their horror they watched as the mare moved forward and sideways, bumping into my chair and knocking the chair and me over to the ground. They quickly took the horse to her stall, righted my chair and helped me up off the ground and into my chair. They kept asking me, 'Are you okay?'"

The volunteers were worried that Debbie had been hurt. But instead of being shaken up, Debbie was angry with the situation, not the horse. She did a quick self-examination to see if everything was okay. "I did a test of my chair to make sure it was functioning properly and nothing was broken on me or the chair. We seemed to have come out unscathed, but the mare had won. We had to use scissors to finish her beauty treatment," she said. Without the buzzing clippers, the horse stood quietly to be trimmed.

Teresa recalls, "I tried my hand at being barn manager for a while, and I think I must have begged Debbie to take it from me. I was such a miserable failure at it. Debbie was awesome, though. She never forgot to order grain, she had no problem sending back crappy hay, her vaccination records were always up to date, and she was nice to our small herd of boarders. I don't recall it being hard for her, but I imagine that the physical aspects of it could have been pretty challenging. The old barn wasn't easy to get around in, and a lot of the tasks were physical. She was always so good at recruiting the right help, too. When the hay was delivered, there was always a ready set of volunteers to unload, whereas I was never able to convince anyone that throwing hay was worth it!"

Debbie put in a lot of time working and volunteering. However, some of her greatest contributions came from her role on horseback at TRC. Her perspective as a disabled rider offered direct and honest feedback that taught the volunteers and staff lessons they would never forget.

Although the volunteers were able-bodied, they didn't necessarily have the right mindset for understanding disabled riders. Once when they were lifting her and manipulating her body on the horse, Debbie yelled, "Stop! I will tell you what to do." She didn't want to be handled without being asked for her input. She also shared her views with staff who would never have thought about the effect of what they were doing because typical students don't usually speak up. Debbie had a major impact when training staff and volunteers, and her special insight elevated TRC's level of service.

18

————

Teaching and taking the lead

After she took on the job of barn manager and teaching the EMTs, it was a natural evolution for Debbie to begin teaching. In her role as an instructor, Debbie saw rewards in every class she taught and could bridge her experiences as a rider with disabilities while teaching others. "I got to understand where some of the students were coming from. I learned patience that I never would have learned, like how much time it takes getting from one place to the next. There was always curiosity surrounding me from students and parents." Debbie said. But she was also careful not to frighten the students.

"I told my students the story of my accident thousands of times but I never used the words 'arena roof'," said Debbie. "I tell them a roof fell on me or I simply say a building fell on me, but never mention the arena. Some of my students are already afraid of horses and I don't want to add another fear by providing extra details."

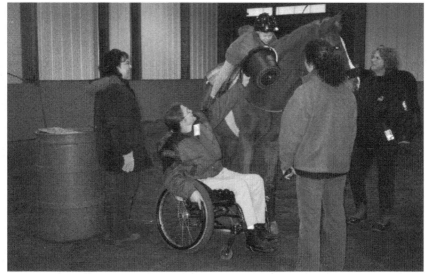

Debbie teaches a lesson.

"I pushed a little harder than some instructors and expected the students to try harder to do things. For example, I had a class of ladies who had Multiple Sclerosis. They wanted to be treated like adults – not babied. I didn't do that to my students, or use politically incorrect wording – that stuff made me nuts, for example – terms like, 'confined to wheelchair'. I also hated being called 'sweetie' and other forms of sympathy, so I didn't do that to my students."

Debbie had a number of weekly lessons and taught the

same morning school groups from the Deepwood Center and Metzenbaum Center. "I worked with senior citizens and little kids and everything in between. I've had some students tell me they relate to me better because of my situation, and in some ways, you can't understand unless you've been through it," she said.

Lynnette Stuart could see that special connection. "Students were inspired by Debbie. She had a huge impact on the program, but particularly because of her perspective as a rider with a disability—she had a special level of awareness for program participants that no other instructor or volunteer had. She also sent the message to students that nothing was impossible."

Did Debbie's teaching style change after the accident? "I don't know that it changed much, I just had to learn how to teach to some of the types of disabilities; for example, teaching a rider who is paraplegic is different than teaching a blind student. But when teaching any beginners, you have to break it down. I remember my fears the first few times I cantered and jumped as a teenager, even though I loved horses. Maybe the wheelchair just makes it easier for my students to relate," she said.

"For people with physical disabilities, knowing how to do it and being able to do it are two different things. I know what it's like wanting to be like everybody else and I can relate," she said.

She has also helped students understand disabilities, for example, answering questions honestly about her wheelchair. She allowed a group of curious students to try her wheelchair through an obstacle course of cones. Then she let them push the chair through the dirt without using the motor, helping them understand the challenges.

Although she had prior experience as a riding instructor, in order to teach therapeutic riding at a facility certified by NARHA (North American Riding for the Handicapped Association), Debbie needed to complete the formal training program, which required intensive study and hours of hands-on experience. She started the program in 1995 and after nearly two years, was able to meet the requirements while simultaneously working and teaching at TRC. She earned the NARHA Registered Instructor Certification in the areas of both physical disabilities and cognitive impairments. The national certification was an important standard for excellence in the growing field of therapeutic horsemanship. At that time, there were more than 500 accredited programs across the United States and Canada.

19

———

The story of Star

On July 12, 1989, Louise Fraser signed the papers to donate Star to TRC. She had contacted TRC founder Kevin Ellison because she was interested in finding a good home where her 16-year-old Morgan mare could also be useful and well-cared for.

"I bought Star when I was in the seventh grade with money I had earned from babysitting. She cost $375 and came from a horse farm where she had been neglected. I learned about TRC when I volunteered there as a young adult when it was based in Newbury. I had seen the care and benefits, as well as what kind of horses they needed. When I was getting ready to go to grad school I needed a good place for Star and remembered TRC," Louise said.

Prior to joining TRC, Star (short for her registered name, "I'm a Star") had been ridden English and Western. She had been a broodmare and foaled several babies; she pulled a cart, jumped and was ridden on trails by children and adults. The little bay mare stood slightly larger than a pony and had a white star on her forehead. After evaluating the mare, TRC determined she would be a good addition to their program and accepted Louise's donation, which at the time put Star's appraisal value at $750.

Louise wrote to Kevin, "I am delighted that you have accepted Star into the program and hope the Center enjoys many years with her." At the end of her note, she added, "I would like to be notified when the Center can no longer use Star so I may retire her to pasture."

Horses in therapeutic riding programs have a slightly different role than in other programs since the central focus of each lesson is the student and his or her needs. The horse is an important part of the team that delivers the riding experience. For this reason, horses are treated seriously and are not toyed with or coddled during a lesson. For example, the horses don't get carrots during a lesson, since it is necessary to avoid distractions. There are strict guidelines for handling the horses to assure they are safe and dependable team members.

In addition to working in TRC's regular lesson program, due to her quiet, dependable nature, Star also was used as a mount for student horse show competitions, as well as demonstrations in volunteer training sessions, and for orientation of new students. She also helped with ground lessons that included teaching grooming and leading horses. She was particularly patient with students leading her from their wheelchairs.

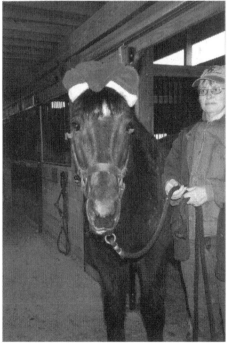
Star dressed up for Christmas.

Reflecting back over Star's career, TRC's current equine manager, Jinene Studzinski, explained why Star was special as a therapy horse. "Star displayed qualities that went far beyond the average horse. She happily tolerated students riding her in all positions – prone, forward, backward, and even sideways. She had helped several students develop confidence through her steady, smooth gait and quiet nature. One student, Matthew, was nervous any time his horse made a sudden movement. He had great difficulty sitting straight on a horse's back. Star would walk steadily despite Matthew's slight lean to the left, and whenever he came too far off-center, she would stop and give him the opportunity to right himself."

Another student who rode Star was afraid that he would not be able to do well with a matching activity that was planned in his riding class. The object was to find a colored cork on the top of a barrel, pick it up, and place it inside a pan of the matching color elsewhere in the arena. When Star walked up to the cork and tried to pick it up in her mouth, the student was so amused that he picked it up himself. He began guiding Star independently across the arena to successfully deposit the cork in the matching pan.

Star was a model therapy horse with a quiet and consistent temperament. During her working career, she allowed gloves to be put on her ears in the winter, as well as plastic antennae and Santa hats on her head, which were fun and gave students focal points for their wandering eyes and attention spans. She let students dress her in costumes on Halloween. Star also taught some riders to canter for the first time. One physical therapist worked with Star while a young rider climbed to a standing position on her back, and then they walked forward so the child could experience the sensation of weight-bearing on both feet and "walking."

Over the years, Star was nominated more than once for NARHA Therapy Horse awards, but never won the honor. However, TRC received a note from NARHA Executive Director William Scebbi: "Therapy horses play an important role in the lives of individuals with disabilities. Their devotion and value to the success of our operating centers is worthy of our recognition... All nominees are winners in the eyes of those who see the daily interaction between horse and rider."

Records on file

A storage room at TRC includes file cabinets of manila folders on every therapy horse in the program, including those who have left. The files are not unlike the personnel files kept by employers that log important work history.

Although the file marked "STAR" didn't contain any NARHA awards, over the years it grew thick with records and other "prizes" earned by the little horse. Clear plastic pockets held artwork, drawings in pencil and crayon that students had made for Star, which once decorated her stall door, as well as photographs of Star with volunteers and students over the years.

Drawing by Carly Presser.

Student artwork decorated Star's stall door. *Drawing by Carly Presser.*

Within the file were dozens of handwritten notes from volunteers to the barn manager reporting care and needs of Star: "Took Star for a walk," "Groomed her and took her outside," "Let her graze on grass and picked her feet." A saddle chart detailed equipment sizes and needs for each lesson as well as student weight limits — 130 pounds early in Star's TRC career, which was reduced to 75 pounds later in her life.

Star's health records for every year included dates of vaccinations: rabies, flu, tetanus, encephalitis, rhino pneumonitis, and more; farrier records of shoeing and trimming feet; and medication for an injured eye and a respiratory check-up. A horse sponsor form from donor Carolyn Hall confirmed she wanted to support Star for another year, funding her care for TRC.

There was a sign on Star's stall door that introduced her to riders. Written in Star's "voice" with her current photo, it read: "I can get a little nippy when you put my girth on, but I stand well for grooming and bathing. Sometimes I may even fall asleep. I am getting older and move slowly so have patience. I turned 30 in March 2003." Although she was well-cared for, Star showed the classic signs of age in a horse with a sagging belly, slightly swayed back, and white around her muzzle. However, her eyes were bright and her ears were alert, showing that she continued to respond to the call of duty as she grew older.

By 2003, after 14 years of TRC service, the monthly usage reports indicated that Star was among the least used of the therapy horses. Instructors were choosing to use other horses in their lessons instead of Star. There were 21 Usage Evaluation forms for Star completed by TRC instructors and staff, including Debbie Gadus, whose own return to the saddle after her debilitating accident had been on Star's back.

"Star was a therapy horse like no other. She will always hold a special place in my heart because she was the first horse I rode after my accident, and she also helped so many others. We could put the most challenging students on her, and she just did her magic. She always stood so still for difficult mounts. I don't think I ever saw her shy or move in a way that would unseat or unbalance a rider. Patient, she did not respond negatively to screaming, bouncing, or kicking students; she helped so many get over the fear they had. I have not met another horse as smooth and steady as she was," recalled Debbie.

There was considerable discussion regarding Star's future. A Horse Evaluation questionnaire gathered staff comments about their use of Star, if they would continue to do so, and if retirement should be considered. The comments were consistently in favor of retiring the mare:

"I try not to use her because she just seems to really be feeling her age lately. I think she has more than earned her gold carrot."

"I do think Star is more tired than when I first came to TRC. No one has made me aware of health problems, however, I want the best for her – whatever that may be."

"I favor semi-retirement (ground lessons and one to two mounted classes a week) but we should continue to watch and evaluate her happiness so we retire her when it is appropriate."

"Star is a great horse to use for ground lessons. I understand with her advancing age she may no longer be suitable for all aspects of our program. It would be sad to see her go but I understand why that may be necessary. She is one of the very few horses still here that was part of the program when I started in 1990. I guess I would prefer to see her retired and living out the rest of her life kicking back in a nice pasture."

Debbie said, "She had done so much for so many I think she definitely deserved some time to relax. She did not appear to be stressed by any of it mentally. But we all look forward to retiring in some way."

After careful consideration the decision was made to retire Star at the end of July 2003, after she had spent nearly half her life serving as a therapy horse. Staff members loaded Star onto the horse trailer and followed the directions on her original donation note, driving out to the eastern countryside of Geauga County.

According to her original owner, Louise, "When I got the call asking me if I wanted to take Star back, I was thrilled. After all those years, I never imagined they would keep my paperwork and contact me, but they did. My husband was a veterinarian, and we had moved to a farm in Chardon. I had two young children at the time, and who would ever have imagined that my childhood horse would become their horse and carry them around another five years."

The mare lived out a very full and happy life, spending many hours in her pasture. Finally, at the age of 35, the day came when she could not stand up in her pasture, a sign that the end was near. "She was down in the pasture and couldn't get up. The kids came down to say goodbye and put a blanket on her, and my husband put her down quietly," she said. A peaceful end to a life well lived by a little horse who touched many lives. She truly lived up to her given name, "I'm a Star".

Louise Fraser with Star post-retirement. *Courtesy of Louise Fraser.*

"There is something about the outside of a horse that is good for the inside of a man."

— Winston Churchill

Part 4

The New Therapeutic Riding Center

20

———

Building a new Therapeutic Riding Center

Fall 1995

In the mid-1990s, the six-county area served by the Therapeutic Riding Center was home to more than 190,000 people with disabilities. Community support for therapeutic riding was gaining momentum as people began to understand the value of the program. The TRC had a waiting list for weekly lessons, as well as the other special programs they offered, including summer camps and vocational training.

By the fall of 1995, TRC proudly announced the kickoff of its "Little Victories" campaign, which needed to raise $3.5 million to build and operate its new therapeutic riding facility. The campaign was named for TRC's role in helping people achieve little victories that have a big impact on their lives. It was led by TRC Board Chairman Joe Mahovlic. He appointed Sunny

Jones the honorary chairman, and she was the first donor to the campaign. Within a few weeks, Little Victories raised $1 million with commitments from the board of directors and a few good friends. Joe and Sunny were dedicated to making the dream of a new barn and home for TRC a reality.

A frozen ground breaking ceremony with lesson horse PC.

After evaluating more than 50 potential sites, the development team purchased 45 acres of former farmland in Bainbridge Township, just miles from TRC's present operation. They planned to break ground once the majority of the building funds were pledged by donors. That put more pressure on the Little Victories campaign to raise another $1 million so they could start building, and TRC's supporters rose to the challenge.

The following fall, the community gathered at an empty frozen field to celebrate the ground-breaking and start of construction on what would be the country's largest center dedicated to therapeutic riding, The new Therapeutic Riding Center would have the capacity to serve more than 1,000 people with disabilities.

While the excitement built, a few miles away TRC continued its day-to-day operations at Salmor Stables. The students, parents, volunteers and staff continued to brave the frigid winter in the drafty barn, dreaming of the heated indoor riding arena and indoor plumbing that were planned for their future.

21

———

Giving guidance

The new facility design was developed with input from staff, local horse professionals, and supporters. Because Debbie Gadus was working as the barn manager at that time, the design team asked for her input as well. "Many of the accessibility features for the new place were incorporated so that a barn manager who used a wheelchair could do their job easily. The equipment in the tack room could all be reached from a wheelchair. All the doorways were nice and wide. Stalls were easy in, easy out. We even chose a new, innovative stall grid that would allow liquid to drain, minimize bedding needs, and allow maximum mobility for wheelchairs. The only place we couldn't afford to make accessible was the hayloft," said Teresa Morris, who was a member of the design committee.

Debbie became involved in planning, researching and analyzing building components and giving input on accessibility issues. The research included visiting other barns to see how they functioned. The TRC plans included many innovative advances, such as a spacious, well-lit indoor riding arena with a watering system to keep down dust and a curtain to divide the arena so that two lessons could be held at the same time. They also planned to install a motorized hydraulic mounting lift to aid students who were unable to climb onto a mounting block. Horse wash racks were designed for people with disabilities who would be grooming or washing horses. They designed classrooms for ground lessons without horses, meeting rooms for gatherings and a spacious tack room that was entirely accessible for those with special needs.

"Debbie's input definitely made us more aware of accessibility issues," recalled Executive Director KC Henry. "For example, because Debbie couldn't reach the top saddle rack from her wheelchair, adjustments were made to the plans. In reality, a volunteer would likely be getting the saddles, but Debbie wanted the ability to be independent. We got a golf cart so she could go out into the field and check the pastures and grounds. She was the reason we put in an elevator to access the upper level. Overall, everything Debbie had to do in her job was harder and in her barn manager position, she recognized her limitations."

22

———

A new home and a new name

Fall 1997

Within two years, the Little Victories campaign raised more than $3.1 million in cash and pledges toward the overall goal of $3.5 million. Construction at 16497 Snyder Road in Bainbridge Township moved along quickly. In November 1997 TRC relocated its program from the rustic Salmor Stables to its brand-new home, a few days before the public grand opening.

A year had passed since the ground-breaking ceremony, and the community gathered once again. But this time, they met inside the brand new 47,000-square-foot, state-of-the-art facility. Luxuries included indoor plumbing, a heated indoor arena, parent and volunteer lounge areas, an elevator and a second-story observation room. The facility was fully accessible and designed specifically to meet the needs of TRCs students.

Because it was one of the largest facilities of its kind in North America, all eyes were on the beautiful farm in Northeast Ohio.

Therapeutic Riding Center under construction.

The President of TRC's Board of Trustees, Bob Crump, was moved by the spirit of the organization and all they had accomplished when he wrote his letter to the community for the TRC newsletter, *Bits and Paces:*

A number of years ago, I had a lengthy conversation with Dr. Stephen Kopits, a prominent orthopedic surgeon at Johns Hopkins Hospital in Baltimore, about people with disabilities. He specialized in treating the orthopedic problems of dwarfs and he had traveled throughout the world in search of dwarfs with treatable problems. He told me that he only had a good reception in the U.S. He said that in most cultures people with disabilities are an embarrassment to their families and thus, are not provided with medical or therapeutic opportunities to improve their condition. Only in America, he said, were people eager to seek ways to improve the quality of life for people with disabilities.

I thought about my conversation with Dr. Kopits when we officially opened TRC's beautiful new facility on November 9, 1997. A number of people asked me before that day why a small organization like TRC, not publicly well known, could raise over $3 million to build and support a permanent new home. I did not have a good answer. I would answer 'how' it was done – how the program was founded, how hundreds of volunteers gave their time to do everything from clean stalls to help train our students to ride horses, how many people made generous gifts. But after thinking about my conversation with Dr. Kopits, it came to me 'why' TRC has been successful is precisely because so many people in our community want to improve the quality of life for those who have physical or mental disabilities. The spirit that made it possible to build a new home for TRC was the same spirit that Dr. Kopits spoke to me about.

For the grand-opening, a special ceremony was held to open the doors to the public. It included student riding demonstrations and tours of the new center. It was the introduction to the world of therapeutic riding for many guests. A parade of students, volunteers, staff and horses marched to a performance of the national anthem sung by student Emily Forquer, after which the audience of more than 450 hushed in preparation for the ribbon-cutting ceremony. All eyes were on TRC's national award-winning therapy horse, PC, as the small spotted equine was led forward to "cut" the ceremonial ribbon, which had been made out of carrots and greens. Right on cue, PC bit into the tasty ribbon, and the crowd burst into applause. At the end of the day, a time capsule was filled with TRC mementos and historic documents, to be reopened 25 years later in 2022.

After 20 years of growing the program little by little, the previously small operation at Salmor Stables was transformed into a major center. By the late 1990s, there were many therapeutic riding centers around the country, and the Therapeutic Riding Center had become common as both a name and a description of the business. Soon after the opening, the decision was made to rename TRC as Fieldstone Farm Therapeutic Riding Center (Fieldstone Farm) to help distinguish it from other centers around the country.

The staff and Board decided that a new facility with a new name should have a formal written mission to define and guide them. After many discussions, they agreed on a brief statement that included the word "disabilities." However, after they posted the statement for everyone to see, it was constantly altered by students and passersby who put an X over the letters "dis" in the word "disabilities." The staff finally conceded, and permanently changed their mission statement to read:

"Through a special partnership with horses, Fieldstone Farm Therapeutic Riding Center offers programs designed by professionals to foster personal growth and individual achievement for people with ~~dis~~abilities." The new mission statement stuck, and helped define the unique nature of the Center.

23

———

Facing change and transformation

The old Salmor Stables facility had little room for growth, while the new Fieldstone Farm had the accommodations that allowed the staff to serve many more students. However, even with all the new benefits and the huge financial investment, there were some things about their old home that people missed.

For example, the close quarters at Salmor presented operational challenges, but it was a sentimental favorite because Salmor was their first dedicated "home" and contributed to the team spirit.

"Everyone was thrilled to be in one place after years of moving to various barns, but Salmor had a family-feel. With only one office, we were physically close and always knew what was going on because we had three desks in the same office. We would all bump into each other but the camaraderie was high.

Parents liked the tiny set up, too, because they could stand ringside during the lessons and talk to the instructors or their child, hanging over a railing that blocked the gate to the riding ring. On one hand, it was disruptive to the classes, but on the other hand, it was well-liked by parents," recalled instructor Lynnette Stuart.

Lynnette Stuart introduces a student to his future lesson horse at Salmor Stables.

"When we moved into the beautiful new, modern facility, it was hard for many people to adjust—both staff and parents. For example, even though there was a microphone to enable people to hear everything in the ring from behind the glass in the observation room, some parents were unhappy because they felt removed," KC added.

To resolve that, Fieldstone Farm started a training program for parents. Once parents were trained as volunteers, they could go into the ring during lessons. For instructors, it was also an adjustment—they were used to watching the horses get tacked up for the next lesson while they were teaching their current lesson. That allowed them to give instructions to volunteers in the barn at the same time they were in the arena. With the new facility, the staff didn't like the fact that the stable and prep areas were removed from the riding ring.

The process of improving and perfecting the final facility design by working out the small glitches continued to evolve at Fieldstone Farm long after the organization moved into its new home.

As an evening riding instructor and last employee on duty, Debbie was often responsible for closing up the new barn and shutting off the lights at the end of the day. However, to get to the light switch box, she had to travel through the narrow, cluttered coatroom. This wasn't a typical place that students moved through, so it wasn't given attention and never tidied up to be made accessible.

The day after a difficult evening, Debbie took the leaders on a tour of the path she had taken the night before. She opened their eyes when she showed them what she had encountered. As was her style, Debbie didn't hesitate to share her thoughts about needing the entire facility to be accessible.

Another time, Debbie took the staff to the student waiting area near the entrance to the indoor arena. There, she pointed to a cork bulletin board laden with paper notices that were held in place by colorful pushpins. "You know what this is if a pushpin falls out? A flat tire on a wheelchair," she said. A few of the staff members saw the board with new eyes as they processed the importance of Debbie's message.

With a larger facility, more students, and volunteers, Fieldstone Farm needed to put more procedures in place to ensure everyone's safety. "As we grew, we had to add more rules and enforce them so staff and volunteers would be accountable. I think that was hard for some people, including Debbie," KC recalled. It was a time of many changes for Debbie.

Once the new Fieldstone Farm was open, the organizers were even more motivated to add programs that would appeal to a wider range of students of all ages. They already ran summer camp and added new activities such as EquiClub, an unmounted program; an outdoor sensory course designed and constructed by a local church youth group and a Youth-At-Risk program that was so successful it served more than twice the expected number of students during its pilot period.

One of the most popular new riding programs was the drill team, which allowed students to practice choreographed group rides. Multiple students performed the synchronized patterns ridden to music. They demonstrated during horse shows, benefit parties and at community events to raise awareness of TRC. The drill team practiced often and Debbie enjoyed riding and participating on the team with the students, as well as volunteers such as Dick Hambleton.

"During one practice, we were cooling off our horses after riding. Before we dismounted, I gave the little bay gelding I was riding a longer rein so he could stretch his head down and relax. Then it happened...he shied at something that caught his eye. He had been a reining horse in his life before becoming a therapeutic riding horse and was very agile to make quick turns, which is exactly what he did. I could not stay with him without the use of my legs to grip and I cursed as I flew through the air, knowing I was going to hit the ground hard," said Debbie.

When a horse gets loose around other horses, it can be very dangerous for the other riders because it can set off a chain reaction. Horses are herd animals and sometimes react by following the leader and running too. Debbie recalled, "They caught my horse and luckily none of the other horses reacted strongly to my horse running to the gate. All of the other riders left the arena and someone put my horse away for me. The drill team instructor brought my wheelchair into the riding arena and helped me into it after doing a once-over to see if I was injured. I seemed okay, but because I came off the horse, and my left leg went straight up to my head, they wanted me to go to the hospital and get checked out. I can't feel pain below the waist, so it is difficult to know if there is an injury."

"Although everything seemed okay, I drove myself to the hospital assuming I would get an X-ray and go home directly from the hospital. When I got behind the wheel in my van, I noticed that my leg did move a little funny and as I got closer to the hospital, I started to feel a little nauseous. 'Oh crap,' I thought, I did break something," Debbie added.

"When I had my original accident that left me a paraplegic, I remembered that during the helicopter ride to the hospital they told me the body's natural reaction to pain is nausea. When I arrived at the hospital after my drill team fall, my fears were confirmed. I had broken my left leg at the femur bone, just below the ball joint and had to have surgery. They put a rod and a plate with screws in my thigh, adding to the hardware that was already in my back. I did heal fairly quickly because I don't bear weight on my legs anyway. I did not miss too much time being away from the farm and was back to work in no time," Debbie said.

She took another fall later when she was riding a horse named Tonka in a lesson. "Once again, we finished the lesson and were cooling out. You would think I would have learned now not to let my reins out so far for the horse to relax. Tonka shied at something outside the arena, but unlike before, it was a slower fall for me. I still went to the hospital to be checked over, but everything was still in one piece. Not long after that, I stopped riding. I was getting older and knew how bad a fall could be, so I decided I had better stick with the driving. Although I still needed my balance for driving, it wasn't the same degree needed as riding," Debbie recalled.

In addition to giving up riding, Debbie made a career decision as well and resigned from her role as barn manager. "When we moved to the new facility, I was afraid I couldn't handle the increased upkeep. At Salmor Stables, we were using volunteer help for the maintenance. There were only 24 horses and we only had a few acres to take care of. We moved to the new farm with much more acreage and a 36-horse barn. How could I take care of all that from a chair in the snow or mud?"

Although she was uncertain of her decision at the time, by not continuing as barn manager, the job change allowed Debbie more time for teaching and to dedicate to a new carriage driving program. That program, which began development at Salmor Stables, would need to transition to Fieldstone Farm and begin serving students as soon as the new facility opened.

24

———

Debbie champions driving

As construction was getting under way at the new facility, the staff began planning new programming. "All new TRC programs developed because there was a champion for them. Debbie really wanted a driving program, and she was a hard worker. During one of our team meetings at Salmor, she brought up her desire for the program. There was already a small therapeutic driving program in existence to guide us, and with Debbie's effort, we got a grant to develop our own program," said director KC Henry.

Debbie was put in charge of special projects and took the lead on development of the new carriage program. She already had proven her abilities overseeing the facility and horses for TRC. Although she had a quiet demeanor, Debbie rose to the opportunity. "I won't take charge, but if you allow me to, I can be a leader," she said as she stepped into her new job.

The long-time dream that Debbie shared with Sunny Jones would allow more people to participate in the equine experience regardless of their ability to sit on a horse or their weight limitations.

"For our therapeutic riding program, there is a rider weight limit of 180 pounds, and this is for the consideration of both horses and volunteers, who are primarily female and who must be prepared to support the disabled riders if they become unbalanced," Debbie said. Many therapeutic riding centers across the country added weight restrictions for the safety of riders, volunteers and horses, making it even more important to offer other non-riding horse activities to keep students involved. At the same time, demand for therapeutic riding programs was increasing among men, due to increased interest from military veterans.

The ability of animals to help humans was documented as far back as the late 1800s, when Florence Nightingale noticed how pets could help reduce anxiety levels in both adults and children in psychiatric institutions. In the 1930s, Sigmund Freud cited the benefits when he used his dog in psychotherapy sessions with his patients and noticed a correlation between the dog's proximity to the patient and the patient's anxiety level. The closer the dog was to the patient, the more relaxed the patient became.

The benefits of animal-assisted activities have proven their value in helping humans, and horses were found to be particularly useful for therapeutic purposes due to their basic gentle nature and their never-ending supply of honest feedback. When a rider is off balance, the horse will move to accommodate it and if the rider doesn't give proper signals, the horse doesn't react properly, which is a helpful teaching tool.

The therapists who served veterans found equine programs particularly beneficial in improving the mental effects of Post-Traumatic Stress Disorder. One of the main motivations behind starting the carriage driving program was to offer alternatives to riding. "Many of the military veterans are men, and the weight limit for riders reduced the potential for NARHA Certified Centers around the country to serve adults until carriage driving was introduced," Debbie said.

Driving horses in harness allowed students to work on balance, coordination, and self-confidence while eliminating some of the physical requirements of the mounted activity. "Driving was also good for the riders who were not comfortable or able to continue in the riding program, or if their instructor was not comfortable with them riding," Debbie said.

In order to teach driving, individuals had to earn the NARHA riding instructor certificate first, which required many hours of teaching experience, and then the NARHA driving certificate. Sunny Jones had been volunteering and supporting TRC for some time, and she joined Debbie in taking the steps necessary to gain her own NARHA driving certification.

"Sunny and I went to the first NARHA driving certification class offered at Shoulderbone Farm in Jarrettsville, Maryland in 1995," Debbie said. They also attended numerous training sessions to complete the requirements. Finally, Debbie earned her driving instructor certification, and Sunny followed two years later.

In later years, Debbie encouraged NARHA to offer the driving certification without first requiring riding certification. "I told them that the true drivers know their horse better than the riders, because they cannot rely on seat and legs to make corrections."

25

———

Driving at Tannerwood Farm

The driving program, which required special horses, equipment, and instructors also needed more space than was available at Salmor Stables, where there wasn't room to drive horses indoors or outdoors, or space to practice driving and train volunteers. Sunny Jones' Tannerwood Farm became a temporary training area for driving until the new facility opened. Sunny offered her farm, ponies, equipment, and expertise to help make the new program a reality. Volunteers split their time between working at Salmor to support the riding program there and training at Tannerwood for the future carriage driving program. The new program would launch after the new facility opened.

Looking back at her own introduction to driving, Debbie recalled, "I first drove a carriage years ago while I was an employee at Tannerwood (before the accident). Sunny taught me with her Welsh pony, Lightning, a little chestnut. He was fun and knew it all. We even travelled out of state for additional training with a pair of young ponies, two bays named Night Captain and Night Wind. We went to train at Top Brass Farm with Jimmy Fairclough who was one of the top competitive carriage drivers in the United States." Fairclough, who was based in New Jersey, would be on the USA's first world championships gold medal combined four-in-hand driving team at the World Equestrian Games in 2018.

During training, Debbie gained knowledge and experience with marathon and cones driving skills, segments that are used in competition around the world.

However, not all of Debbie's early experience was positive. "I knew Sunny's ponies because I spent all of my days caring for them. I tried to train one of them to drive, but he would not have it. We wrecked two breaking carts (used for training horses) trying to learn. He took off and jumped the bar across the indoor arena. Another time, I was out in the driving field and we had finished a nice drive. We were going to cool out when he took off for no apparent reason. I tried to steer him toward the fence to stop, but ended up tipping the cart over. I fell clear and he ran around the field, busting up the cart. We never hitched him after that; he was sold as a riding pony. In hindsight, maybe I should have tried to let him run it out, but if we had hit a hole in the field going that fast, we could have wrecked the cart," Debbie said.

"I don't know that I liked driving any more or less than riding; it was just different, and a good skill to have if I went into the stuntwoman business. I never really considered that seriously, but it did come to mind a few times because I like western movies," Debbie added with a smile.

The Hershey Foundation responded to a grant proposal and awarded TRC funds to purchase a specially designed cart with a ramp to begin the new program. The TRC newsletter, *Bits and Paces*, published a notice that volunteers were being sought and anyone willing to help should contact Debbie.

During the summer of 1996, Sunny and Debbie began working as part of the team of six dedicated driving volunteers who practiced with the horses and ponies, but no carriages. Among the volunteers were Dick Hambleton, Juni Clark, Jane Muir and Sue Harris. During the learning process, they practiced with long lines, walking behind the ponies to become familiar with driving. They worked on training the driving horses, practiced teaching and exercises, and learned about safety and the rules for procedures.

Sunny Jones teaches volunteers details on driving.

While still at the Salmor Farm, they received the perfect donation to launch the driving program – Shadow, a Standardbred who had prior driving experience on the harness race track as a youngster. In his earlier life before TRC, Shadow's registered racing name was Darrel's Shadow. Foaled in 1981, his father (or "sire," in horse terms), was named Butler, and mother ("dam") was Wilma C. Reed. During his racing career, the diminutive bay Standardbred was a trotter pulling a sulky, or racing cart, and earned a total of $35,261. Like all race horses, he was tattooed for identification on the inside of his upper lip.

When his racing career ended in 1990, Shadow became a

pleasure horse, ridden English and Western by children and adults. He was 16 when he went to TRC on trial as a driving horse in June 1996. After being tested under many conditions over a four-month period to confirm he was suitable, Shadow was formally donated to the program. Owner Patricia Waliga made the decision to let Shadow go, and his value at the time was listed at $500. To TRC and the driving team, Shadow was priceless—he was the cornerstone horse who built the new driving program.

After he was accepted into the program, Shadow was moved to Tannerwood where volunteers could practice driving him until the new facility opened. He was the perfect size for the TRC cart and went to work with the volunteers who practiced their harness fitting, driving skills and techniques for getting students into the carriages.

Sunny donated additional funds to purchase the first wheelchair-accessible cart, the Bennington Superstar from England. Not long afterward, a Bird-in-Hand carriage was purchased from an Amish craftsman in Pennsylvania.

Everyone worked together to get the driving program ready to launch, and the extra effort united Debbie, Sunny, and their strong supporter, Dick Hambleton.

26

———

Meet Volunteer Dick Hambleton

The first volunteer to sign up for the carriage program initiative was Dick Hambleton. A retired chemical engineer who had served in the Army during World War II, Dick volunteered for many community activities. They included the theater where he helped as an usher, and as a member of the Lake FarmPark Volunteer Mounted Posse, where he patrolled trails, conducted demonstrations, trained horses, and rode in parades.

After he began volunteering at TRC, Dick wanted to commit all his time there, so he became a regular fixture. Over the years, he helped train and prepare horses for lessons, served in classes as a side-walker and leader, and even rode on the drill team.

Dick and Debbie had developed a strong working relationship since Debbie's initial visit to TRC in 1994. After that first lesson, when Dick handled Star, their relationship evolved and became more collaborative. They were often paired in the lessons Debbie taught, and Dick worked leading or side-walking. His style worked well with hers. While some volunteers would help the students too much, Dick understood the importance of allowing the students make mistakes so they could learn from the experience. "I won't let them run into a wall, but I will let them run over cones," he said.

Debbie drives Shadow with volunteer Jessica Alcorn.

Over the years, he helped students accomplish many goals. For some, it was speaking for the first time or gaining strength to walk. For others, it meant building confidence to inspire them to do more in their daily lives.

"Dick helps students accomplish as much as they can by gently nudging and encouraging them. He is a wonderful person," Debbie said.

When Debbie and Sunny started driving training at Tannerwood, Dick had been volunteering with TRC in the riding lessons for eight years. Tannerwood provided a quiet place to learn, away from the riding classes that were being conducted at TRC, with enough space outdoors. They could practice on trails as well. As they worked to get the program ready to launch, the team enjoyed the relaxed environment, and there was a close sense of family.

Dick's wife, Carol, also helped at Tannerwood and sometimes watched the training when she brought their infant granddaughter to visit, adding to the family-feel. Everyone, including Debbie, took turns holding the baby.

The driving program required more volunteers than the riding program did in order to make sure it was conducted properly. The instructor was ultimately responsible for everything that happened in the ring, in addition to conducting lessons for the students. Other well-defined volunteer roles also required specific training.

For example, the job of the able bodied (AB) whip (a whip

is a term for a driver) involved being in the carriage with the student. The whip would do as much or as little as the student needed in controlling the horse and preventing accidents. Some students did most of the driving, but others needed the AB whip to take control if they got fatigued or started to get into troubling situations. Sometimes they would remind students of the instructions verbally or do a little hand-over-hand, aiding them directly with the reins. The AB whip is always the first one in the carriage and last out at the end of the lesson.

The header is the volunteer who stands at the horse's head in therapeutic driving, holding a lead rope attached to the horse's halter for such tasks as mounting and dismounting. Spotters and student assistants watch for things that might become a problem and help the students mount and dismount. For students in wheelchairs, this can be a lot of work and take some time.

Carriage driving was formally added as a program after the new facility opened and word of mouth helped it grow. Dick volunteered solely in carriage driving. Serving as an AB whip, he got to know many of the driving students.

Butch and Barry were two of the first students in the driving program; both had joined because they reached the weight limit for riding but wanted to continue at Fieldstone Farm. Butch, who suffered a brain injury, and Barry, who had cerebral palsy, were both in wheelchairs. They began driving reluctantly because they enjoyed riding more. Barry participated, but never as happily as Butch, who was glad to do anything that meant he could be around the horses.

Driving allowed students to improve their body trunk stability and balance, hand and arm strength, motor skills, and coordination, as well as improve their range of motion and stamina. Games and scavenger hunts were incorporated into the lessons to help meet educational goals and have fun.

"Jamie was another driver we worked with early on. She was a wheelchair user who came from the Deepwood Center in Mentor. She didn't ride because of her deep fear of horses that kept her from getting close enough to get in the saddle, but she would get into the carriage and drive. After a few months, she finally got close enough to pet the horse," Dick remembered.

He developed his own way of working to meet the needs of each student. For example, one boy insisted on calling the horse Brownie, even though Dick regularly used the correct name, Shadow, and would say, "Walk on, Shadow," each time they would drive the carriage forward from a stopped position.

Each student left his or her own impression on Dick. "I had one student who was a blind veteran who attended from a local hospital. When I gave him the reins to drive, I would tell him when we were approaching a corner and advise him to pull the left rein and helped him do so. It made him so happy because, although he couldn't see, he could feel the difference of traveling in a corner." One day Dick said, "Want to go faster?" and told the veteran to trot. He was thrilled to be in control, and it was a real treat for Dick to share his experience.

Small program, big impact

"Driving was a small part of our overall programming and took a lot of space at the farm, but it made a big impact. The overall program had a waiting list of riders though, and when there was a driving lesson in the ring during the winter, it took up the space of two group lessons that might have been running at the same time in a split ring. However, in the summer, driving could run outdoors, and that worked well," said KC as she watched the program progress.

Debbie did most of the day-to-day work to keep the driving program running. She ordered the carriages and harnesses, managed equipment maintenance, handled the training with

Sunny's help, scheduled driving volunteers and decided which students they could accommodate. The driving team also planned for the program's ongoing expansion.

The construction of a mile-and-a-half carriage trail around the spacious new farm was completed in 1999. When Fieldstone Farm proudly hosted the annual NARHA national conference that year, more than 600 attending from around the country had a chance to see all that they had built.

Debbie and Dick Hambleton in the new tack room.

After years of planning and construction, a public grand opening for the carriage trail was held. Sunny and her husband,

Ted Jones, had contributed greatly by donating the funds to build the trail and had the honor of cutting the ribbon to officially open it. Immediately after the ribbon cutting, Debbie pulled forward in a four-wheeled carriage over the bridge and through the cut ribbon, driving a horse named Durango. The dedication ceremony was followed by hayrides to view the loop trail while guests celebrated with food and bluegrass music.

That same year, 22 years after TRC launched with eight students, Fieldstone Farm Therapeutic Riding Center served more than 600 riding and driving students. Volunteers donated more than 22,000 hours that year, and the farm's operating budget reached the $1 million mark, putting the program among the top three in the nation.

27

A parent's perspective

Jeanne Sydenstricker was working and living in California with her husband, Mike, and their two sons, Stephen and Brent, when the boys were diagnosed with a rare chromosomal disorder that was later identified as Fragile X. Although Stephen was hyperactive and speech-delayed with a lazy eye at two years of age, the doctors weren't able to diagnose the condition until he was six. When Brent wasn't talking at age two, Jeanne knew there was a problem. The boys participated in a clinical trial testing for Fragile X, and Stephen and Brent were among the first to be diagnosed with the disorder. Fragile X presents as a wide range of disabilities which can have minimal impact or be completely debilitating, making the carriers unable to do things for themselves.

Jeanne understood from her own upbringing the value of

horses in a child's life and had been looking for a horseback riding program for her boys when she was introduced to therapeutic riding.

"I had grown up riding and wanted to be able to take my family on trips to a dude ranch. I really wanted them to enjoy horses and riding. We found a vaulting program (gymnastics on horseback), which the boys did for about a year and a half, but we weren't excited about it," she said of the limited options available for them to be involved with horses.

"I had a friend at work who wanted to start a therapeutic riding program. We agreed she would handle the riding portion of the program and I would get the people and certification done," Jeanne said. Her job at TRW Inc. was to handle program management for billion-dollar satellites, so the organizational work to develop a therapeutic riding program was right up her alley.

The women successfully launched the Ride to Fly program in Palos Verdes, Calif., which is still operating today. "It is a very small program. A parent asked me, 'Why do you do it?' and I explained, if I can create something, it should be available for anyone who needs it, not just my own family," Jeanne said.

A few years later, the Sydenstricker family relocated to

Ohio for her work. "We were looking for a good place to raise our kids, especially since they are kids with disabilities. TRW President Peter Hellman was instrumental in helping us make the decision where to move after we said we wanted to be away from Los Angeles and somewhere in the Midwest," she recalled.

Stephen and Brent were able to start riding again in Ohio, and the family discovered Therapeutic Riding Center. At the time, TRC had just launched a capital campaign and committed to building a new dedicated facility, but the lessons were still being held at Salmor Stables.

As he grew older, Stephen eventually weighed 180 pounds, which limited his ability to ride. That weight is significant at most therapeutic riding centers because it is the size limit given to riders for the safety of the volunteers who work as side-walkers, as well as for the well-being of the horses. Stephen had a choice of going on a diet to reduce his weight or entering TRC's new carriage driving program, instead of riding.

"I fought the weight restriction but couldn't do anything about it. I even considered going somewhere else, but I knew we were well taken care of, respected and loved. Although that may not be unique among nonprofits, the breadth with which they do things at TRC is very special," Jeanne said.

One of the riding activities Stephen hated giving up was the drill team for independent riders. The team members met once a week in addition to their riding class and practiced walk and trot patterns that were set to music. They had an opportunity to perform in front of the public for special events, such as Lake FarmPark's Disability Awareness Day.

"I don't remember when we first met Debbie Gadus, but I do know how important she became as Stephen's driving instructor," Jeanne said, referring to the time when Stephen transitioned to the non-riding program.

From the beginning, she recalled that Stephen loved everything about the driving program. "Stephen likes horses and driving, but a huge part of the program is the environment. People accept each other as they are. For him, the lessons helped with communication, listening to instructions, and following directions to carry them out. Attention span is a big basic, and I describe his focus like a string of Christmas lights where some are flickering. Exercises such as going through a cones course without knocking over one of the balls requires focus, and you can see your results when you see one ball fall. The instructors use positive reinforcement like, 'atta boy' but there is instant reinforcement when you see what you are doing and get a reaction from the horse," said Jeanne.

Debbie's influence

"Debbie is a powerful message to students. She leads by example. I remember several horse shows when Debbie rode. Her smile was beautiful. I was astonished to see she could do it. Marvelous. She wanted to do it even though it was very hard for her to sit up on her own. She could go where she wanted to go," Jeanne said.

"Students and veterans have tremendous issues, and she knows this is life, and you make it as good as you can. I didn't know Debbie before her accident, but it is a unique experience going through what she did, learning to live through disability and having a full life in spite of it. It has to impact her ability to relate to others. She is a naturally reticent person, and I am not sure her connections with the students would be as instantaneous with an instructor who is more outgoing, or if Debbie's ability to connect with her students was enhanced by her disability," Jeanne said. "No matter how she was hurting, or how hard it was for her, as an instructor Debbie always focused on the student. If I asked Stephen if Debbie was in a wheelchair, he wouldn't have known. It wasn't part of her. She was just out there doing her job like anyone else."

"I enjoy talking with her, even though she is a reluctant conversationalist. Reluctant when talking about herself, but not talking about horses, driving, the carriage trail...that, she is comfortable with," Jeanne added. There wasn't time to talk much during the lessons, but Jeanne could visit during annual awards ceremonies and TRC outings at Tannerwood where she got to know Debbie better.

Jeanne noticed that as a teacher, Debbie never asked a lot of detailed questions about her students' disabilities. "She never really wanted to hear details about that. Maybe that is why it is wonderful that she accepts them as they are and deals in an appropriate way in that hour she is working with them. For example, when Stephen isn't on his game, it's obvious —he's chattering, looking at everybody. He is distracted. Debbie has developed an intuitive sense of how she needs to work with people in that moment. She relates and is observant and doesn't rely on files or records from the past," Jeanne said.

At the new Fieldstone Farm, parents are able to watch lessons from a second floor observation room. Jeanne and Mike liked seeing what Stephen was learning. From the observation room, they could see and hear because Debbie needed to speak loudly for the driver to hear. There was playful interaction between Stephen and Debbie as she would let him know if he wasn't doing something right, but always in a positive, sometimes humorous, way while teaching.

Involvement between the parents and instructor, and the student's doctor if physical issues are involved, is an important element of the therapeutic program. Everyone works together to define the goals for each student and what is critical for them to gain, in addition to having fun. As a team, they measure the changes along the way and assess how the student is doing, with instructors providing feedback on progress and issues during class. That feedback was important to Jeanne and Mike so they could address problems that were identified.

Fragile X is on the autism spectrum, so the ability to focus is something they worked on through therapeutic riding and driving. "Stephen could hear the feedback, and that helped him absorb what he was hearing. He loves the positive social interactions," said Jeanne.

"Stephen loves the program and talking about the horses. Right now, Mitch is his favorite horse and May is another favorite. He talks about Jewel, who is new and he will say, 'She was feisty' or 'She didn't want to work'. He likes that they aren't all perfect," she said.

Over the years in the program, Stephen became very involved. The staff let him do extra work such as hitching up the carriage in advance of his lesson. "It's important to him because he likes to be in control. He wants to come a half-hour early or stay late. For Stephen, that extra time is great; we appreciate that they allow him to do the extra work and that he is physically able to help, but he really wants to be with the horses more than anything," she added.

When the weather was too hot or cold and the riding or driving portion of the lessons had to be canceled, students had classroom learning opportunities instead.

"During a span in the winter, there were three weeks when they couldn't ride or drive. Stephen had been there for 20 years and didn't want to do a ground lesson to learn about tack or feed or learn the parts of the horse at his stage in the program. He already knew all about the horses and parts of the carriage," Jeanne explained.

"Brent, my other son, was very different. When we used to go on vacation to dude ranches, Mike and Brent would walk along while Stephen and I rode," Jeanne said. "He fought us about going to Fieldstone Farm and was sneezing and itching with allergies. He was just miserable and didn't feel an affinity for horses. He stayed with the program for five years, and we kept thinking we could give him allergy pills and he would get into it eventually, but no."

Stephen Syderstriker competes in Riders with Disabilities events during the Chagrin Hunter Jumper Classic horse show. *Anne Gittins Photo.*

"Debbie would fight and cajole him, but she couldn't get him to participate. Brent can't express himself with language," explained Jeanne. "His reception is fine, but communicating complex thoughts verbally is a problem, and he just stops and won't do it. Debbie tried to convince Brent: 'Take your time... take one step...move a little closer, the horse will wait.' One or two times we gave in and stopped, but we didn't give up on the program overall. But it is expensive if you aren't interested, and we paid for our own lessons monthly, about $50 each lesson."

After Brent reached the weight limit and had been driving for a year they discontinued his lessons, but Stephen continued with a passion. Today Stephen and Brent are adults in their 30s. Stephen still visits Fieldstone Farm weekly. He would like to go more, but he also has a daily job working in a warehouse, packaging, sorting, and labeling. His other activities include guitar, book club, and play practice. "He is interested in everything and only limited by my money and willingness to drive," Jeanne said with a smile. "I had to put the brakes on all the activities because he can be exhausting. At night, he wants to go to the gym and play basketball."

Jeanne continued her involvement with Fieldstone Farm as well. After she stopped traveling for work and retired from her job, she served on the board of trustees, advising Fieldstone Farm and helping the organization reach its goals. "When I became a board member, it taught me an incredible amount about how a good board should run," she said.

She knew the board's fundraising efforts were particularly important so that students and families who needed financial assistance could get support. "Fieldstone Farm provides help in the form of riderships, which are like scholarships. Lessons are offered at a discounted rate due to the generosity of donors who contribute money. The funds we raise are used to pay for lessons, the cost of programs, or horse expenses and more," she said.

As a parent, what does Fieldstone Farm Therapeutic Riding Center mean to Jeanne?

"Number one, I wanted a place the boys could be with horses, so I was happy for them. Most important is that I know Fieldstone Farm has the best interest of my family and entire disabled community at heart through their programs and innovations such as veterans' programs, the driving program, and Gaitway School for students who are not successful in a traditional high school. For me, they are an example of what a nonprofit that serves the disabled should be. They have strong benefactors, and the reason people are passionate is because they do meaningful, quality service."

"I have learned that success is to be measured not so much by the position that one has reached in life as by the obstacles which he has had to overcome while trying to succeed."

— Booker T. Washington

Part 5

Continuing to Grow

28

___

National Recognition

1997

As Ohio's tiny Therapeutic Riding Center transformed into a multimillion-dollar facility, the North American Riding for the Handicapped Association (NARHA), founded in 1969, also was growing fast. By the mid-1990s, here were more than 500 NARHA centers, with various equine-assisted activities to benefit people with special needs. Among the centers, Fieldstone Farm Therapeutic Riding Center had earned a reputation as a leader in the field. Several members of the Fieldstone Farm team had been honored with awards from NARHA. In 1992, the lesson horse, PC, had been named National Therapy Horse, and the following year, Executive Director KC Henry was honored as NARHA National Director of the Year.

In the years following Debbie's accident, she had

demonstrated her resilience by returning to riding and building a new career working at Fieldstone Farm managing the barn, teaching, and developing the new driving program. In 1997, NARHA recognized Debbie's accomplishments by naming her the Adult Independent Rider of the Year in her region of the country. Debbie learned of the honor in advance and was invited to receive the award at the NARHA annual meeting and convention, which was being held that year in Denver, Colorado. The annual meeting was a big event because it was the only time representatives of all the NARHA member centers, their instructors and teams got together.

Debbie traveled to Denver accompanied by her mother and several staff members including Jane Muir, Teresa Morris, KC Henry, and Lynnette Stuart. The conference was held over several days and included meetings and workshops, along with the annual awards dinner. Although the trip was challenging logistically and it was exhausting to meet so many people and be so busy, Debbie juggled the excitement with her nerves, unaccustomed to being so active.

"I attended seminars, a regional meeting, driving meeting, adult independent riding meeting, and we went out to eat one night," Debbie recalled.

When the evening of the awards banquet came, Debbie shared the spotlight with other honorees and received her award in front of representatives from NARHA centers across the country.

From left: Rose Gadus, Debbie, KC Henry and Jane Muir
at the PATH Intl awards.

"The award was for being a rider with disabilities and doing something with that," Debbie explained simply afterwards. "In my case, it was for getting certified and teaching others with disabilities and being the barn manager. Some of the honorees have overcome great odds to ride again. Some compete at the national level, which is out of the ordinary. Today there are many categories of awards by regions and age ranges, but at the time, that was the only riding award given," she said proudly.

In future years, Debbie cheered on her teammates as NARHA continued to recognize members of Fieldstone Farm Therapeutic Riding Center team with well-deserved awards. The following year, when the conference was in Boston, Sunny Jones earned the Regional Volunteer of the Year award and the year after that, it was Dick Hambleton's turn to be in the spotlight as the 1999 Regional Volunteer of the Year. That was the year the national conference was held in Cleveland, less than 30 miles from Fieldstone Farm.

More than 600 NARHA members from around the country traveled to Ohio. A portion of the conference activities were held at Fieldstone Farm Therapeutic Riding Center. The staff worked hard to prepare the Farm for the big event and proudly hosted tours to showcase their center and programs, including the driving program.

29

World Disabled Driving Championship tryouts

Competitive sports for the disabled were expanding around the world due to the growth of the Special Olympics, and horse sports were no exception. Although Debbie worked around horses and had become an accomplished driver and driving instructor, it had never been her ambition to compete. However, when the opportunity came along, she answered the call.

In 1994, the first American team of disabled drivers competed at an international driving event in Hartpury, England. The event was an unofficial demonstration of drivers with disabilities from six nations, and the United States went home with the team Silver Medal. The U.S. drivers included Mary Gray, Cindy Goff, Tom Turner, and Rebecca Merritt. Gray also won the individual Gold Medal.

Since that demonstration, the United States continued to

promote driving for the disabled, and in the spring of 1998, it began the process of fielding a team for the first official World Championships for Disabled Drivers in Wolfsburg, Germany, which would be held the following year. The Championships were expected to draw teams from 10 countries, but the top contenders were Germany and Great Britain. The U.S. team tryouts were held in Maryland at Sybil Dukehart's Shoulderbone Farm.

That facility was the home of the United States Driving for the Disabled organization, founded in 1982 by carriage driver Sybil Dukehart. Her inspiration came from officiating at Britain's Royal Windsor Horse Show, where she became aware of the programs for handicapped drivers and decided that Americans also could benefit. She went on to start a therapeutic driving program at her farm and imported two modified carriages from England that could accommodate the disabled drivers.

Debbie was one of five drivers who visited Shoulderbone Farm to compete for a place on the three-person American World Disabled Driving Championship team.

"I'm not totally sure whose idea it was to invite me to try out, but this was before the Paralympics and they were trying to get driving added. I must have gotten on somebody's mailing list,"

Debbie said.

"This was the same Maryland farm where Sunny and I went to attend the first NARHA driving certification class in 1995, so I think they may have remembered and contacted me when they were looking for more people to compete. At the time, I was working as the special programs coordinator at Fieldstone Farm and as an instructor of riding and driving, and I was still taking riding lessons myself."

Driving at Tannerwood Farm. *Courtesy of Sunny Jones.*

Sunny Jones had submitted a letter of recommendation for Debbie to be considered for the team. In her letter, she detailed Debbie's experience with pleasure driving, training at Top Brass Farm, practice at Tannerwood, and limited local show experience.

Sunny wrote, "We both realize the need for experience in competition, and as her coach I feel she is ready and anxious to gain that experience. I know that being considered for the team is a great honor and privilege and will also be a major commitment, but Debbie will thrive on the challenge and do her best to meet the requirements. I know she would be a good team member."

"Sunny took me to the tryouts with at least four volunteers from Fieldstone Farm, including Dick and Carol Hambleton. I was never a horse show person and I always screwed up when I was being judged. I would pick up the wrong lead or something. I was much better at training and teaching than competing," Debbie said.

For the World Championships, the drivers used borrowed vehicles and ponies and competed over a weekend in dressage and cones to test their precision on Saturday. The following day, they drove a trail course in the marathon to test skills over distance and through obstacles. Because of poor weather, the marathon course was shortened. In addition to the challenges of the course, driving unfamiliar carriages with an unfamiliar horse or pony added to the difficulty faced by the contenders.

Debbie drove a four-wheeled carriage with a 13.2 hand Welsh-Haflinger pony mare named Sweet Adeline. At home, Debbie was used to driving a two-wheeled vehicle and a larger Standardbred horse. Although she had ordered a four-wheel vehicle with a hydraulic lift for her Fieldstone Farm driving students, she wasn't accustomed to driving one at the time.

Spectators, including members of the media, learned Debbie's story as well as the story of Ohio's Fieldstone Farm Therapeutic Riding Center. It was just at the time that Fieldstone Farm was beginning to offer driving, so attention for the program was very important.

The competition was won by Mary Gray. The Maine driver also had been a winner at the 1994 driving Championships. Second place went to California's Michael Muir, a seasoned driving competitor. Third place was Kate Rivers from Florida who became the third member of the team for the World Championships. The final two drivers, fourth-placed Cindy Goff from Kentucky and Debbie, in fifth, were named alternates for the competition in Germany.

"I wanted to do well, as it would bring more recognition to Fieldstone Farm and I was disappointed that I did not make the team. But I do not show well and was very nervous. It was my first and only combined driving show but maybe someday I will do another," Debbie said, happy to have had the opportunity to try out in such good company.

Later that year, the first official International Para Equestrian Committee World Championship for Drivers with Disabilities was held with nine teams. The United States team won the bronze medal and Kate Rivers took the individual bronze.

30

———

Traveling and serving beyond Fieldstone Farm

Debbie was accustomed to travel by car and plane; however, traveling was always a challenge, even though people were always willing to offer assistance. She shared a typical air travel experience: "I get help going through the airports and get to board the plane first. Once I get to the entrance of the plane I have to get a tag for my chair at the gate. They stow it with the luggage and hopefully it comes back in one piece. I usually get an aisle seat and when others in my row board, they have to crawl over me to get to their seats. Some people wait for me to stand up expecting me to get out of their way and I have to tell them I can't. Then after we land, I am the last one off the plane, which means if I have to make a connecting flight, I need to schedule extra time to get from one plane to the other and hope there are no complications. Getting a taxicab that is wheelchair-accessible takes a bit of exploring or calling around.

"At the hotels, you have to hope the person taking your reservation knows that there is a difference between handicapped accessible and wheelchair accessible or there can be a whole new set of issues to deal with," she explained. "A room that is handicapped accessible has grab bars by the toilet, enough room to move around with a walker and usually a tub bench in the bathtub. A wheelchair accessible room has wider doors, a raised toilet and grab bars, room below the sink to roll under, a roll-in shower, and usually one bed so there is more room to move around the room."

Teresa Morris. *Courtesy of Lake Erie College.*

As Debbie became more involved in serving on various NARHA committees, she traveled to more meetings and conferences around the country. One person who often came with her was Teresa Morris, who shared her own road warrior stories.

"It is certainly an educational experience to find out that 'handicapped accessible' has a wide range of meanings. I had no idea."

Once Debbie and Teresa went to Indiana for a NARHA regional conference with therapeutic riding centers from that area of the country. By then, Debbie had become a pretty savvy traveler and knew the barriers of traveling in a wheelchair, so she prepared well before her trips and asked all the right questions in scoping out the conference venue with the organizer, who was a therapeutic riding professional. The Indiana conference presentations were held at a local therapeutic riding center with the expected mobility challenges. However, the Saturday night dinner was planned to be held off- site in a church basement.

Teresa recalled, "*A Basement*! This triggered a set of very specific questions, and before the trip I heard Debbie on the phone asking them. Apparently everything checked out, because we left for Indiana with a colleague, Jane Muir, at the wheel. Debbie has this great chair that the wheels pop off and the chair folds up to fit in the trunk. She rode shotgun, and Jane and I got as quick as any NASCAR pit crew assisting her. The conference went smoothly, and Saturday, we moved to the church for dinner. The first thing Debbie saw as she rolled up to the church was a set of about 20 steps. Upon inquiry, we learned this was the only way into the church, but they provided handicapped accessible accommodations. The 'accommodation' provided was two burly but well-intentioned men who didn't even stop to discuss their plan with Debbie. They just lifted her chair with her in it and carried her directly up the stairs. It was over before anybody realized what was happening. Debbie, however, was hyperventilating while trying to put on a brave face."

It was particularly ironic that such barriers would be present at a NARHA meeting of professional people who work with and understand the needs of people with disabilities.

"Next, we had to get to the basement. No problem. Just find the elevator or ramp... Oh no. No elevator...no ramp. The stairs to the basement did have a chair lift. One of those things you see advertised in the *Reader's Digest* that rides a rail up and down the edge of your stairs. Debbie gamely transferred into the chair and was very conspicuously deposited to the bottom of the stairs where she had to wait for her chair to follow. This was all accomplished with maximum help from the most people possible in the most public setting imaginable. Not the picture of independence that Debbie so faithfully pursued, but she was game," Teresa said.

In addition to her travels, Debbie was also getting more experienced in her leadership role and running meetings. In order to launch the driving program at Fieldstone Farm, she had written the driving rules and compliances for the program and made sure that they met the national driving standards. The compliances are the accreditation requirements that official site visitors will review when they observe a program and see in writing. When the program was fully operational in 1999 and Debbie and Sunny were the driving instructors, a new Fieldstone Farm Driving Committee had been established to oversee and advise the program. The members of the committee were strong and outspoken in providing guidance on horse selection, training, and procedures. Although it was a challenge at times to lead, Debbie learned to manage the strong personalities on the committee, speaking up and expressing herself, rather than holding back on her opinions and letting her frustration build up.

Shortly after the program started, the Fieldstone Farm Driving Committee was already expanding it and looking for a second quiet driving horse and more volunteers for the intensive driving training program. By summer's end, they had four students in the program. As the program grew, Debbie's role shifted from managing the driving at Fieldstone Farm to helping the national association develop its new programs. At times, Fieldstone Farm hosted national visitors to tour their facility and see their programs in action, as well as learn from the staff.

Teresa shared a story of such a visit. "One hot and sultry August day, some NARHA industry leaders, two highly-respected certification evaluators, visited the farm for a certification, and they asked for a separate meeting with Debbie to consult on some proposed driving standards.

"A terrible storm blew in as we sat down in the big meeting room. We could see the arena doors blowing straight in on their hinges due to the wind. The noise was tremendous and the electricity was flickering. At one point, the front door blew open and slammed shut, causing a pressure change so significant that some of the tiles of the drop ceiling in the room displaced.

Our hair stood on end. Everyone but Debbie moved quickly to a side wall anticipating a building collapse."

Minutes later, when the storm subsided, Teresa asked Debbie why she wasn't scared. She answered, "No way would a building collapse on me a second time! I'm not that lucky!"

Debbie became a valuable source of information for NARHA centers around the world that were starting driving programs, as well as the national organization where she helped write policies and procedures for the universal program standards.

When she was approached to join the national driving committee for NARHA and take a lead role, Debbie realized the work would require more meetings, but she knew it was an important opportunity she wanted to pursue.

Now that there were enough people involved in running the driving program, Debbie decided the time was right to make a change and resigned from her full-time role at Fieldstone Farm.

"I could never have been doing what I was doing while running the driving program. Working on the committees and traveling to Florida, presenting programs on disabled driving, and continuing to represent Fieldstone Farm for NARHA at conferences all took a lot of time.

"I really focused my time on NARHA – it is a wonderful

organization," she said. When she could, she would fill in for Sunny as a driving instructor at Fieldstone Farm and attend staff meetings and functions on an infrequent basis as time permitted.

"Sunny and I were the first to become certified in the NARHA driving class before we started working on setting up the standards for the program. That is when we met Molly Sweeney, Mary Wolverton-Morgan, and Sybil Dukehart at her place in Maryland (which later hosted the disabled team tryouts), along with others who served on NARHA committees.

As a membership organization, NARHA operated with committees, policies and standards that were created by therapeutic riding volunteers from around the country. The volunteers also took on committee assignments with the aid of the NARHA staff members. While she was serving as a member of the driving committee, and later as its chairman, Debbie began working with staff member Michael Kaufman, director of education and communication for NARHA. He became a strong influence in her life.

"As a committee leader, Debbie was quiet and reserved and did not overpower people. She had to learn to speak up and to referee others. She did get to a point where she would put an end to a conversation or discussion in a very clear, but still subtle way. Her shy nature brought out the best in others, who never felt threatened by her and wanted to succeed 'with' her. She had the respect of her colleagues at all times. All in all, a great combination," he said.

Michael and Debbie had a very good working relationship, and he helped her when the time came to make her first presentation, speaking to an audience of NARHA members at the national conference.

"I was a nervous wreck," Debbie recalled. "The topic was "Starting a Driving Program" and included what you and the instructor needed to get certified. The audience was people thinking about starting a driving program, and I shook through the whole thing," she said.

"What I first noticed about Debbie was her deep shyness and absolute fear of speaking publicly, to the point of sometimes being quite anxious. It might have been natural to respect that projection and to leave her alone, but at the same time, don't ask me why, I felt that she wanted to be pushed and challenged," said Michael. He looked past her anxiety and began working with her, asking her to do more presentations at conferences and write articles to fully serve the role for which she had volunteered.

"Each time she appeared, Debbie was overwhelmed and appeared to be doubting herself, but then she just did it and showed amazing capacity, great ideas, good instincts. She had really good group leadership skills at conferences and committee meetings, in the articles she wrote and the standards she helped refine and create. She was a master at follow-up, and what she says she will do, she does. It was just very nice to work alongside her, to watch her become more confident on the national stage and to get recognized for the unique life experience and talents she had to offer," Michael added.

"What surprised me most about Debbie was her unexpected sense of humor. It was under the surface, but she is actually a very funny person and can laugh at herself. I do remember very well the dryness of her humor and sometimes a hint of sarcasm in her voice," he said of the way Debbie could make a point.

Debbie's work went beyond the NARHA driving committee. Her knowledge as an adult riding student and work as an instructor at a therapeutic riding center were unique and very valuable as NARHA tackled even more challenging issues. Debbie began working as a member of the Adult Independent Rider Committee.

"The committee started largely because of a woman named Evelyn Refosco, who at the time was on the NARHA board. Evelyn used a wheelchair due to a car accident. She and a few others felt that the perspective of adult riders was not reflected in the NARHA governance structure or program service delivery. They rallied around Americans with Disabilities Act (ADA) issues, making the point, 'not about us without us,' a very current and new issue of inclusion then," Michael said. Debbie was a natural to serve that committee.

"One of the challenges in the field of therapeutic horsemanship was that it was often able-bodied individuals representing and speaking 'for' persons who actually have the experience of living and riding or driving with a disability. Within NARHA, there was a group of adult independent riders who all stepped up to point out that their perspective often was not really included or recognized. One reason for this also had to do with the large number of children served by NARHA centers, and adults habitually speak 'for' children," he explained.

In the early days of growth in therapeutic riding and setting the standards for NARHA center development, these adult independent riders asserted themselves and actually formed their own committee. According to Michael, "The instructors and other 'currently abled' leaders in NARHA initially weren't aware that they didn't truly understand the many needs and desires of persons who have a disability. Some of the challenges are semantic, such as the difference between a woman 'in a wheelchair' vs. a woman 'using a wheelchair.' Other issues are social. For example, a standing person talking down to a man in a wheelchair, forcing him to look up from a weaker and lower position rather than the standing person seeking a chair and making the conversation more equal. Or much more bluntly, a person treating an individual with mobility issues as if they were developmentally delayed. Debbie was part of that (adult) group as well, bringing in her own experience."

"We were trying to help instructors understand and educate people within the industry by making improvements for adult riders," said Debbie. In one effort, the committee explored how many riding centers were accessible by wheelchair and worked to educate and promote expanding accessibility.

"Debbie's perspective on mobility, her knowledge of horsemanship, and her drive for excellence earned her a much-respected voice in the therapeutic horsemanship industry. Her approachability and dry wit encouraged discourse and discovery," Michael said.

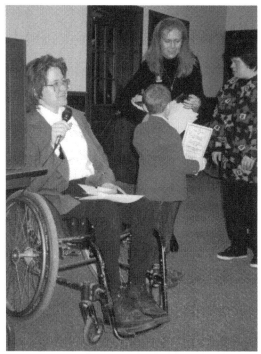

Debbie announces while Jennifer Ball presents student awards
at Fieldstone Farm

In 1999, Debbie was once again recognized for her contributions to the field when she was awarded the NARHA Sis Gould Driving award for her work with both the driving committee and Fieldstone Farm. Named after longtime driving advocate Sis Gould, who founded the High Hopes Therapeutic Riding Center in Connecticut, the award recognized NARHA members who exemplify outstanding dedication to the promotion of carriage driving for individuals with disabilities.

Although receiving a certificate of honor from this national organization meant so much to Debbie, when she looks back and shares her fondest memories, she is still drawn to one letter in particular. It is a souvenir from a talk she gave to a local middle school during its annual Special Abilities Day. Sixth graders at Kenston Middle School in Bainbridge Township heard about Debbie's accident firsthand, and she told them about living with a disability. After the talk, Debbie received a thank you note from the school, and it included several letters from students sharing what they had learned. Among them was one from 12-year-old girl who wrote:

"Debbie Gadus is a very influential person. She has inspired me to have determination and never give up. Debbie has shown me that if you really love something, you will always go back to it. It takes a great deal of courage to be severely injured in a barn, then go back to riding. My goal is to be as courageous as Debbie someday."

31

———

Guest speaker

2017

The classroom was on the first floor of the Lake Erie College George M. Humphrey Equestrian Center where the stables, riding arenas, and some of the classes were held for those majoring in equine topics. It was a simple classroom with tables and chairs and a tabletop podium at the front of the room, a computer and pull-down screen, and a white board. The Principles of Therapeutic Horsemanship class was meeting, one of the courses mandated for students enrolled in Lake Erie College's newest major, Equine Therapeutic Horsemanship.

Teresa Morris, the former program director of Fieldstone Farm Therapeutic Riding Center, was an adjunct faculty member in the Lake Erie College School of Equine Studies and instrumental in the development of the three-year-old college program. She taught two classes, one of which was Assisting with Therapeutic Riding. Like Gretchen Singleton's class in the 1970s, this course offered riding lessons for community riders with disabilities, and Lake Erie students assist by leading and side-walking. The other class, the Principles of Therapeutic Horsemanship, was a semester-long class offered every two years, and when it was held, Teresa invited Debbie Gadus to speak.

When the course was once again offered in 2017, there were about a dozen students waiting for Debbie to begin her 90-minute lecture. Debbie opened her PowerPoint presentation* on the screen to the title page introducing the ADA, or Americans with Disability Act, and explained the law that had been passed in 1990 to ban disability discrimination. She focused her talk on the section of the law dealing with public accommodations, such as having an accessible entrance and access to goods and services, as well as restrooms and other details.

Debbie explained how a riding facility needs to be structured so that a disabled student or guest can have full accessibility according to the ADA. The information was a compilation of what she had shared with Fieldstone Farm TRC when they were building the farm, as well as all that she has learned over

*Debbie's presentation notes are included in Appendix A, on Page 245

the years as a rider and instructor with disabilities.

At one point in the course, the students had to design their own centers, which is why she went into such detail on public accommodations. Debbie focused more on dealing with people with disabilities and tried to answer any questions as she presented the information.

A student's hand went up, "What places do you find the least accessible?"

Debbie answered, "Private homes, historical areas, some restaurants, and some doctors' offices."

As she explained the issues with public accommodations, Debbie wheeled her chair around and demonstrated with her own body how wheelchair users need extra room to open doors, move under tables or counters, and reach things in front of them versus the side. She gives the students visuals as to what the ADA requirements are and why they are in place. Before the college was remodeled, she actually took the girls into the restroom to show them how she could not get her chair into the stall.

As she moved through her lecture, Debbie spoke about each section of the ADA, explaining how therapeutic riding centers need to be fully accessible so those with disabilities can enter, park, and move around. In the goods and services section, she detailed the need for people to be able to function with or without assistance and the need for signage and controls, as well as counters, seats and tables that are accessible. Every area of the facility must be made accessible with ramps, lifts, or elevators.

She could see the students nodding and their eyes opening wider as they considered the details. She knew they would look differently at restrooms, sinks and water fountains moving forward. These are amenities they took for granted and never viewed as a challenge for those with special needs.

Debbie looked around the small classroom and directly at each of the students as she offered them an insider's perspective of the reality of living with a disability and what her peers and students with disabilities would want others to know about how to look at and talk to them. As the lecture came to a close, students finished their note-taking, some using paper and pen and others typing directly into their laptop computers. Debbie prepared to wrap up the lecture as the clock neared dismissal time.

"Words have power," she said, reminding the students to put people first. "Avoid terms like victim, suffers from, afflicted, confined to wheelchair, and wheelchair-bound to define or describe people with disabilities."

Debbie Gadus.

It had been nearly 40 years since Gretchen Singleton taught the Riding for the Handicapped course at Lake Erie College and Kevin Ellison sat in that class gathering ideas before starting his own pilot program. The course ended when Gretchen left Lake Erie College to pursue other work and space became an issue with running the therapeutic riding program at the college. However, since those early days, the field of therapeutic riding had taken off and grown considerably, prompting the comeback of Lake Erie College's therapeutic riding curriculum.

As Debbie prepared to leave, she wheeled through the Equestrian Center lobby, noticing a copy of the current *Lake Erie College Magazine* lying open on a table. The page was turned to an article announcing their new therapeutic horsemanship major: "The major combines practical coursework in equine studies and health, riding courses, and riding instructor training with courses in business management and education. Students are building their skills and experience to prepare for a wide variety of positions in the equine therapeutic industry."

32

———

Heading Home

By herself in the Equestrian Center parking lot, Debbie noticed it was about to rain. She had parked her old van nearby so it would be easy to load up after class. She pressed a button on the automatic entry fob on her key chain and the ramp descended from the van so she could wheel aboard and reposition herself behind the steering wheel. The drive home was only 20 minutes and she took her time thinking about the day, the students, and home.

As she drove into her lane and up to the house, Debbie could see her long-time friend and fiancé, Harold, in the window as he was getting dinner ready and their cat, Zeus, watching him intently. Their 15-acre dream farm finally had become a reality.

She bought the ranch house with some of the money from her disability pay and even had a horse of her own once more. One day, when she was at Fieldstone Farm, she made the mistake of saying "I like that horse," as she admired him from afar. She got a call when Tonka was retiring, and Debbie took him home.

"Today we still have a barn and pasture, although it has been a while now since Tonka passed away and we have not gotten another horse," she said. "Maybe someday."

Harold is the love of her life. They met after her accident when Debbie had gone out with friends to a local hangout called Twisters, which was attached to a Dutch restaurant. Harold was out to dinner with friends for a fish fry and was playing pool afterwards before he came over to say hello and meet Debbie. They ended up dancing to country music, she from her wheelchair and he right alongside, and they continued to see each other after that chance meeting.

"He makes me laugh, and there are not many people who can do that. Fifteen years later we are still very much in love," she said of the man who is ready to help if she needs it, but knows to wait until he is asked.

"There is no greater agony than bearing an untold story inside you."

— Maya Angelou

Afterword

33

Everyone has a story

Fieldstone Farm Therapeutic Riding Center.
Tammy Packer for Fieldstone Farm.

2018

I climbed the steps to the second floor viewing area to watch the carriage driving lesson in progress below. The viewing lounge was empty, and I looked out through the wall of two-way glass to the arena. I was fascinated by the imprints in the indoor sand footing. Wide carriage tracks wound in patterns around the ring, punctuated by human and equine footprints around the wheel patterns. Then I noticed another set of tracks, smaller and softer than the carriage tracks and wondered what had made that pattern. Then, of course, I knew.

The instructor for this lesson was Debbie Gadus. I watched her four-wheeled electric chair move smoothly across the arena floor, cutting the narrow pattern as she tracked the progress of the four-wheeled carriage being driven by her student, José. Beneath a green ballcap I could see the rim of her glasses and firm-jutting chin as she focused on the carriage and gave occasional instructions and encouragement. Dressed in khakis, a hoodie, gloves, and heavy beige work boots, Debbie prompted her wheelchair control pad, smoothly pulling parallel to the carriage.

Sitting next to José in the driver's seat was the able-bodied whip who was ready to assist if necessary. The carriage was being obediently drawn by a small quiet palomino Haflinger horse named Mitch who moved slowly as directed, weaving through the colored cones in a wide serpentine pattern.

I walked back down the steps to the ground floor lobby to see if I could get a better view of the lesson. A woman was squeezed up against the glass window of the door watching and taking a video on her cell phone. "That's my son," she said with enthusiastic pride. "He's been doing this for a month. One day, he's hoping to ride a horse. This is a good way for him to get started." She went on to describe how, in addition to driving the carriage, José pets the horses and helps brush them before and after the lesson to get comfortable with the 900-pound animals.

After I introduced myself and explained that I was writing a story about Fieldstone Farm's 40th anniversary, I asked the mother if she would answer a few questions. She nodded and continued to talk; her eyes never left her son. I learned that José is a 99-pound, 20-year-old college student. Since being diagnosed with leukemia when he was 13, he has battled the effects of chemotherapy that resulted in the need for a kidney transplant, hip replacements for his damaged bones, diabetes and chronic pain. "We're grateful he's alive and thankful he received a good kidney. We met the family who donated the kidney after the father died in a car accident," she said.

"José is amazing to survive everything. The chemo cured him but destroyed everything in his bones." She went on to tell me that José wants to be a child psychologist one day and help other kids through tough times. College is hard for him though, and the other students aren't as helpful as they were in high school, when they assisted him with his backpack around campus.

The mother, Pat, and her son learned about Fieldstone Farm

Therapeutic Riding Center from a friend at their church who volunteered there. From their urban Cleveland home on East 185th Street, it is about a 45-minute drive to the rural country setting. "I really like the drive out here because it's so scenic and free from houses. José settles down on the drive after he takes his pain meds. I am glad he is feeling better. He's going to do big things one day."

As I thanked her and turned away from the indoor arena, I saw a bright yellow school bus pull up outside the front doors to Fieldstone Farm. A dozen students walked slowly toward the bus from the North wing of the facility where the Gaitway School has been housed for the past 12 years. The first high school in the country located at a therapeutic riding center, Gaitway has its own full-time principal, specially trained and certified teachers, job coaches, and a licensed social worker. A total of 68 students have graduated since Gaitway opened in 2006 and most would not have made it through a traditional high school environment due to their emotional or behavioral issues. The low Gaitway student-to-teacher ratio helps students become successful and receive the personalized education that they need. The name incorporates a play on words, using the spelling "gait" meaning movement instead of the traditional spelling for "gateway".

Instructor Lauren Simak prepares for a driving lesson.
Tammie Packer for Fieldstone Farm.

The last time I looked at Fieldstone Farm Therapeutic Riding Center's numbers for my story, there were 1,300 students annually, including 200 veterans. Each week, there are 250 volunteers working. Fieldstone Farm owns 35 therapy horses, also dubbed four-legged heroes in the horse world. Long-time riding instructor Lynnette Stuart, who was there for Debbie Gadus' first lesson when she returned to the saddle after her accident, is now Fieldstone's chief executive officer.

Although Debbie officially left her full-time job at Fieldstone Farm in 2006, she continues to volunteer as a driving instructor one day a week. She also volunteers to train the driving horses and teach new driving assistants in the program. On occasion, she will substitute for another instructor and see some of her old students.

As I headed through the lobby, I passed Ernest, a military veteran, on his way to the barn. I asked how he is and tell him I saw the video and article about him in Fieldstone's newsletter. "You're a star," I teased him, and he beamed, but I can tell he is a little embarrassed by the recognition.

Ernest is not afraid to share his personal story to help others understand the value of therapeutic riding and driving. For years, his life was going along smoothly and he was happily married with children and grandchildren, running his own company and playing golf and skiing in his free time.

Then one day that changed after he tripped on a curb and an old foot injury from Vietnam came back to haunt him. The pain from his foot radiated to his back, making it difficult to walk and even stand up straight. He couldn't work or do the things he loved, and depression took over his life as memories from the war came flooding back to the point of suicidal thoughts haunting him. "I had never really processed my feelings from Vietnam. I was in denial," he said of his form of Post-Traumatic Stress Disorder.

At one point, he became agitated after a flashback, and it scared his grandson. It was at that moment that Ernest knew he needed help. He reached out to counselors at the Veterans Administration (VA) and learned about the program with Fieldstone Farm. "I remembered my days growing up on a farm in Georgia as the oldest of five kids and I was intrigued. I enrolled in the program and spent two sessions as a student working with horses and the counselors from the VA. The program, one of the largest equine programs for veterans in the country, helps veterans come to terms with their feelings as well as gaining physical strength, attaining success beyond what they could achieve in a traditional counseling office setting. Coming to Fieldstone allows me to take a vacation from my chronic pain and heal both physically and mentally. They have transformed my life! When I am here I focus on my abilities, not my disabilities."

Ernest volunteers for one of Debbie's driving classes. He is always there early and has everything laid out and ready to go before the class begins. "He is great to work with and I love his sense of humor. We laugh a lot together, especially when I am not so clear with my instructions," Debbie told me.

As a volunteer, Ernest enjoys helping others find confidence, courage, and independence, just the way he did as a student at Fieldstone. For example, once when he was volunteering he helped a veteran who is a triple amputee hold the reins while carriage driving, and together they both felt joy in the accomplishment.

Ernest, a military veteran, takes Sonny for a walk.
Creed Woodka for Fieldstone Farm.

As I talked with Ernest in the lobby, other volunteers stopped to say hello. While visiting I learned there was recently a celebration for Sunny Jones, who retired as a volunteer driving instructor. She continues running her summer camp, Chincapin, which is now based at Tannerwood, and visits Fieldstone on occasion.

I also heard that our friend Dick Hambleton had to stop volunteering at the age of 96 due to vision problems resulting from a stroke. Former Program Director Teresa Morris was in the process of relocating out of state with her family. Although some of the people I interviewed have moved on, so many new people have joined the team and are carrying on all the programs and more.

I looked back through the window into the arena as Debbie's lesson was wrapping up. It reminded me of a conversation with Teresa when I had trouble explaining Debbie's complex personality. Teresa gave me a wonderful description: "Soft like steel. When you look at her, you know she's sitting in a chair, her manner is unassuming. She's soft-spoken… but look at what she's done. Built the driving program. Built herself a house. Built herself a family. Goes wherever she wants. Does whatever she wants. On her own terms. Propelled by her own arms."

Fieldstone Farm Therapeutic Riding Center has earned its reputation as one of the top centers in the nation. As I've worked on the details of the story to honor their 40 years of operation, it's been hard to know where to start writing because there are so many amazing stories inside this single center. One thing is certain - the work at Fieldstone Farm is sure to continue long past its 40th anniversary.

Volunteers and students enjoy a trail ride.
Marty Culbertson for Fieldstone Farm.

Notes and Resources

Appendix A

Debbie's presentation notes on Working with Persons with Disabilities (Lake Erie College lecture)

Everyone is different, even if they have the same diagnosis. Generally use common sense and treat them as you would anyone else. Offer to shake hands (left hand shakes are acceptable) and relax. (It's okay to say 'see you later', 'did you hear about this', 'running in circles', etc.)

Be Polite - People with disabilities want to be treated like everyone else. Show a person with disabilities the same respect you would expect.

Communicate - Talk to the person with a disability, not their companion, and use appropriate language. Do not scream. If you are going to be talking for a long time, get down to their level if they are in a wheelchair.

- Announce who you are, as well as those who are with you, to a person who is blind.
- Give a light tap on the shoulder of a person who is deaf to get their attention.
- Wait for a person who speaks slowly to finish the sentences, and ask questions that can be answered briefly or with a shake of the head.

Offer Assistance, then wait for the answer. Listen to the instructions. Do not be offended if they say no.

Visual Disabilities
- Speak to a person who is blind the same way as anyone else, in a normal tone of voice.
- Introduce yourself.
- When conversing in a group, say the name of the person you are speaking to.
- Let them know what is going on in the environment (everyone is laughing because...).
- When you move/leave let them know so they are not left talking to "empty air."

Assisting

- May I help you?
- If they accept: They will take your arm.
- Giving directions - be specific.
- To help them to a seat, place the person's hand on the back or arm of the chair.

Guide Dogs - Obtain permission before talking to or touching them; they must stay focused when in harness.

Hearing Disabilities

- Gain their attention.
- Find out how best to communicate.
- Talk to the person.
- Use body language.
- Use paper and pencil.
- Sign language.

Lip reading − It is only 30-50 percent effective. Speak normally with short sentences and be patient. Make sure there are no physical barriers and the environment is quiet and contributes to the success of lip reading, which means no food in your mouth or covering your mouth with your hand or a long mustache. No background noises like radios, machinery, or a lot of other people talking, which will interfere with them being able to hear what they can if they just have an impairment.

Speech Disabilities − There are many causes. Give your whole, unhurried attention and move to a quiet area. Be encouraging and ask questions with short answers. Find out if writing is an option.

Cognitive Disabilities
- Use clear, specific language
- Condense lengthy directions into steps and use short, concise instructions
- When giving verbal information, pause appropriately for processing time
- Use visual images to reinforce
- Use concrete language and limit use of sarcasm

Epilepsy - Seizures

- Keep calm and do not restrain the person
- Clear the area of harmful objects
- Keep crowds back
- Do not force anything between the teeth
- Stay with them afterward as they may be confused

Wheelchair Etiquette

- Relax and make eye contact
- Sit down when possible
- Offer assistance but wait for the answer and listen to directions. Ask how to help and make sure the person is ready

Appendix B

———

Chagrin Valley Therapeutic Riding Center
Fieldstone Farm Therapeutic Riding Center

Timeline 1978 to 2018

1978 Kevin Ellison launched Chagrin Valley Therapeutic Riding Center with weekly lessons for eight students

1979 Program moved to Dorchester Farms. Horses trailered in for group and private lessons

1984 Name changed to Therapeutic Riding Center (TRC), Inc. Expanded to serve students outside the Chagrin Valley

1985 Instructor KC Henry became the first paid employee. Lessons held twice a week

1988 TRC moved to Lake FarmPark where they held a Special Olympics the next year

1990 Expanded to serve 119 students. Moved to Salmor Stables in Newbury, leasing five stalls

1991 Gained national recognition from NARHA (North American Riding for the Handicapped Association) when Ellison was named Regional Volunteer of Year

1992 Leased all of Salmor Stables for classes serving 141 students. KC Henry (TRC Executive Director) elected to National Board of NARHA and "PC" named National Therapy Horse. Plans developed to build dedicated therapeutic riding facility

1995 Little Victories fundraising campaign began with goal of $3.5 million to build and endow a new facility. Summer camps and hippotherapy program launched

1996 Training for future driving program began. Land purchased for new facility

1997 Grand opening of new facility in Bainbridge Twp.; new name announced: Fieldstone Farm Therapeutic Riding Center (FFTRC) to replace Therapeutic Riding Center (TRC)

1998 Carriage driving trail constructed; sensory course added

1999 Fieldstone Farm Therapeutic Riding Center hosted the national NARHA conference with more than 600 attendees from around the country

2000 FFTRC programs grew to serve more than 600 students

2001 Lynnette Stuart named FFTRC Executive Director

2006 FFTRC opened the Gaitway High School for at-risk youth from school districts across Northeast Ohio; 710 students served in various FFTRC programs

2007 Veterans program started at FFTRC; 800 students served by FFTRC programs

2011 NARHA (North American Riding for the Handicapped Association) changes its name to Professional Association of Therapeutic Horsemanship International (PATH Intl.)

2018 Fieldstone Farm Therapeutic Riding Center celebrates 40th anniversary

Appendix C

———

Glossary of Terms

From PATH Intl. Standards for Certification & Accreditation 2018

Therapeutic Riding Terms

ADA – Americans with Disabilities Act, signed into law in 1990, which provided the world's first comprehensive civil rights law for people with disabilities

Arena – a working space defined by structural barriers used for program activities

Center – a structured organization that provides equine-assisted activities and therapies to persons with or without disabilities

Competition – individual or team sports at the local, regional, national or international level; integrated or specialized competition that can be breed- or activity-based

Driving – activities related to carriage driving. May be considered equine-assisted therapy if driving activities are incorporated by a therapist into a treatment plan. May also be done in competition.

Equine – a general description inclusive of horses, ponies, mules, donkeys or miniatures

Equine Activity – any activity that involves an equine

Equine-Assisted Activities (EAA) – any specific center activity, e.g., mounted, driving, vaulting or ground activities, grooming and stable management, shows, parades, demonstrations, etc., in which the center's clients, participants, volunteers, instructors and equines are involved

Equine-Assisted Therapy (EAT) – therapy or treatment that incorporates equine activities and/or the equine environment. Rehabilitative or habilitative goals are related to the client's needs and the medical professional's standards of practice.

Facility – the premises at which the center conducts its activities and business including buildings and grounds

Header – the person who stands at the equine's head during halts who is responsible for keeping the animal relaxed and still

Hippotherapy – a physical, occupational or speech therapy treatment strategy that utilizes equine movement. This strategy is used as part of an integrated treatment program to achieve functional outcomes.

Lift - a mechanical stationary or mobile device that facilitates the transfer of a participant from one place to another

Organization – an administrative or functional structure (as a business or association)

PATH Intl. Certified Instructor – an instructor of therapeutic horsemanship who is certified by PATH Intl. at the registered, advanced or master level or who holds an approved adjunct certification

Professional Association of Therapeutic Horsemanship International Member Center – a center that has established membership with PATH Intl. and agrees to comply with PATH Intl. Standards

Therapeutic Riding (TR) – therapeutic horsemanship that involves mounted activities including traditional riding disciplines or adaptive riding activities conducted by a Professional Association of Therapeutic Horsemanship International Certified Instructor

Therapist – in the United States, a licensed, credentialed physical therapist (PT), occupational therapist (OT), speech language pathologist (SLP). Outside of the United States, those licensed/credentialed therapists and health professionals who have met the criteria to legally and independently provide comparable services within their state, province or county. A therapist is one who specializes in the provision of a particular therapy, a person trained in the use of physical methods, such as exercises, etc., in treating and rehabilitating clients to overcome physical impairments.

Therapy – specific treatment that meets requirements for third party billing, or billing for services with a third party may be provided by a licensed/credentialed professional such as a PT, OT, SLP, psychologist, social worker, MD, among others. Licensing/credentialing laws differ by state.

Volunteer – unpaid individual who, under the direction of the center administration, assists with the ongoing activities of the center

Driving Terms

ABW (Able-Bodied Whip) – a whip with the skills to drive a horse and vehicle unassisted. These skills include a minimum of 50 hours of driving experience in various terrain and conditions and complete knowledge of harness and vehicle terminology, competencies in managing emergencies. The ABW will hold a second set of reins while the driving student enters and exits the vehicle. The ABW will assist with the second set of reins as needed during the driving lesson.

Bit – the metal attachment to the bridle that goes into the equine's mouth, used to control the equine

Blinkers – a pair of leather or rubber eye cups attached to the driving bridle to limit rear vision and keep the equine's vision focused forward

Breastcollar – the part of the harness that fits around the chest of the equine and against which the animal exerts pressure in pulling a load

Breeching – a harness strap that goes around the equine's hindquarters to help hold back or stop the vehicle on a downgrade

Bridle –consists of a headstall, bit and reins for guiding an equine

Cart – a two-wheeled driving vehicle

Carriage – a four-wheeled driving vehicle

Collar – pad going around the equine's neck, accommodating the hames to which two traces are attached, an alternative to a breastcollar

Crupper – a padded leather strap that goes around the base of an equine's tail and is used to keep the harness in place on the equine's back and keep it from slidng forward

Halter – a bitless headstall for tying or leading an animal

Harness – noun: the assemblage of leather or synthetic straps and metal pieces by which an equine is attached to a vehicle, plow or load; verb: to attach an equine with a harness to something such as a carriage

Header – a trained equine handler who stands at the head of the equine with an attached lead line whenever the equine is standing still. A header is required while the equine is being put to or taken from the vehicle, while participant is entering or exiting the vehicle and available whenever assistance with the equine is needed.

Impairment – any abnormality, partial or complete loss of, or loss of the function of a body part, organ or system

Instructional Driving – driving that involves the participant holding the reins and learning how to drive

Lead Rope – a rope with a snap on one end that is used to lead the equine

Participant – the driver with a disability; client driver

Putting To – the process of attaching the equine and driving vehicle to each other

Saddle – a padded part of a harness worn over an equine's back to hold the shafts

Spotter – a trained assistant on foot in the driving area who watches for a possible problem and is prepared to take immediate action

Turnout – a driving vehicle with its equine(s) and whip

Vehicle – any device that conveys people and objects over land. In driving, this may be a two- or four-wheeled vehicle or a sleigh with runners.

Whip – preferred term for the driver

Appendix D

Resources and reading

Interested in learning more? Check out these websites and organizations related to disabled riding and driving:

American Hippotherapy Association:
www.americanhippotheraphyassociation.org

Canadian Therapeutic Riding Association: www.cantra.org

Disabled Drivers Association: www.disableddrivers.weebly.com

Disabled Sport USA/ Riding: www.disabledsportusa.org

Equestrian Therapy: www.equestriantherapy.com

Equine Assisted Growth and Learning Association:
www.eagala.org

Federation of Horses in Education and Therapy International: www.hetifederation.org

Horses and Humans: www.HorsesandHumans.org

Professional Association of Therapeutic Horsemanship International: www.pathintl.org

Riding for the Disabled Association of United Kingdom: www.rda.org.uk/

United States Driving for the Disabled: www.usdfd.org

United States Para-Equestrian Association: www.uspea.org

Check out these websites and organizations related to youth and equestrian:

United States Equestrian Federation: www.USEF.org

United States Dressage Federation: www.usdf.org

The United States Pony Clubs: www.ponyclub.org

4H Youth Clubs: www.4-H.org

Interscholastic Equestrian Association: www.rideiea.org

Intercollegiate Horse Shows Association: www.ihsainc.com

National Collegiate Equestrian Association:
www.collegiateequestrian.com

The American Youth Horse Council: www.ayhc.com

Author Notes

I first heard about Debbie Gadus' accident when she made front-page news. The story stayed with me because it was a freak accident, and I thought about it as I worked in my own barn and rode that winter because it could have happened to anyone in Northeast Ohio. But the story of what Debbie did with the rest of her life interested me even more.

I learned later that we are related – Debbie's grandmother, Sophie, and my grandmother, Stella, were sisters who emigrated from Poland and grew up in Cleveland. Our fathers were cousins. Debbie and her family would have been just as happy if they weren't called upon to share details of their lives but I thank them, and in particular, Debbie, for sharing her experiences.

When I started to write about Debbie, her story intertwined with two other organizations I knew well. I studied at Lake Erie College and attended my friend, Gretchen Singleton's

Riding for the Handicapped class, where Kevin Ellison was also a student. And over the years I volunteered my public relations services to support The Chagrin Valley Therapeutic Riding Center, which evolved into Therapeutic Riding Center and eventually Fieldstone Farm Therapeutic Riding Center. Knowing the subjects helped to fuel my writing and desire to tell their stories; as I spoke with the people involved and delved into my research, I came to realize how well the pieces of these stories fit together to form *Little Victories*.

Acknowledgments

While I spent countless hours researching facts through newspapers, websites, newsletters, and files, this book is built on personal interviews with individuals who were willing to share their stories and observations. In addition to Debbie Gadus' contributions, special thanks to Lynnette Stuart, Sunny Jones, KC Henry, Teresa Morris, Dick Hambleton (who passed away in January 2019), Jeanne Sydenstricker, Jinene Studzinski, Ernest Jordan, Maureen Foster, Louise Fraser, Michael Kaufman, Cami Blanchard, Kaye Marks of PATH Intl, and numerous students, parents and volunteers who provided background.

Thank you to the photographers who helped me tell this story: Tammie Packer, Creed Woodka, Second Story Productions LLC, Anne Gittins, Lynn Ischay, Mike Levy, and Maribeth Joeright. Many of the photos in the book were provided courtesy of Fieldstone Farm Therapeutic Riding Center as well as Cheff

Therapeutic Riding Center, the Gadus family, Sunny Jones, Lake Erie College, News-Herald, and The Plain Dealer.

I am so thankful to my friends behind-the-scenes who shared their talents to help me with this project: Flo Cunningham, Nancy Jaffer, Karly Keirsey, Gail Kucharik, Esther Morgan, Sarah Wilsman, Michelle Wood, Elizabeth and Dennis Yurich.

Special thanks to my husband, Dave, for his support and critical editing, and my daughter Claire. Claire edited countless drafts over several years of pulling this book together including outlines and proposals. She provided invaluable support and encouragement through the rewrites, rejections, and road blocks.

About the Author

An equestrian since her youth, Betty Weibel's career spans more than 30 years as a journalist and public relations professional. She researched and published her first non-fiction book, *The Cleveland Grand Prix: An American Show Jumping First,* with The History Press/Arcadia in 2014. The lifelong Ohioan starts each day in her barn caring for her horses, including a retired therapeutic riding pony. For more information visit www.bettyweibel.com.

End notes

1 Sabrina Eaton, "One Dead, two hurt as roofs collapse in Geauga," *The Plain Dealer*, January 18, 1994

2 Tammy Stables "Buried Alive, they found ways to cope," *The News Herald*, January 22, 1994

3 Tammy Stables "Barn Roof Collapse Traps Two," *The News Herald*, January 18, 1994

4 Ibid.

5 John Dickey, "Roof Collapse Kills Teen-Ager in pool," *Star Beacon*, January 18, 1994

6 Connie Shultz Gard, "Buried alive, Emily recited a fairy tale," *The Plain Dealer*, January 22, 1994

7 Sabrina Eaton, "One Dead, two hurt as roofs collapse in Geauga," *The Plain Dealer*, January 18, 1994

8 John Dickey, "Roof Collapse Kills Teen-Ager in pool," *Star Beacon*, January 18, 1994

9 Sabrina Eaton, "One Dead, two hurt as roofs collapse in Geauga," *The Plain Dealer*, January 18, 1994

10 Connie Shultz Gard, "Buried alive, Emily recited a fairy tale," *The Plain Dealer*, January 22, 1994

11 Ibid

12 ibid

13 ibid

14 Tammy Stables "Buried Alive, they found ways to cope," *The News Herald*, January 22, 1994

15 Connie Shultz Gard, "Starting all over again," *The Plain Dealer*, February 3, 1994

16 Tammy Stables "Buried Alive, they found ways to cope," *The News Herald*, January 22, 1994

17 ibid

18 ibid

19 ibid

20 Ibid

21 Ibid

22 Connie Shultz Gard, "Starting all over again," *The Plain Dealer*, February 3, 1994

23 Fieldstone Farm Therapeutic Riding Center, "25th Anniversary 1978-2003," power point presentation

24 ibid

25 Professional Association of Therapeutic Horsemanship International website, pathintl. org/about-path-intl/history

26 Ibid

27 Fieldstone Farm Therapeutic Riding Center, "25th Anniversary 1978-2003," power point presentation

28 Alan Achkar "Back in the saddle again," *The Plain Dealer*, January 22, 1995

29 ibid

30 ibid

31 ibid

32 *Bits and Paces*, 1995, vol. 3

33 *Bits and Paces*, 1996, vol. 2

34 Bob Crump, "From the President's Desk," *Bits & Paces*, 1997, vol. 3

35 *Bits & Paces*, 1997, vol. 1

36 Fieldstone Farm Therapeutic Riding Center, "25th Anniversary 1978-2003," power point presentation

37 Lorraine Ernst, "Animal-Assisted Therapy: An Exploration of Its History, Healing Benefits, and How Skilled Nursing Facilities Can Set Up Programs," Annals of Long Term Care: Clinical Care and Aging, 2014

38 *Bits and Paces*, 1995, vol. 3

39 Wendy Jones, "Borrowed Ponies Help Choose Disabled Driving Team," *Chronicle of the Horse*, May 1, 1998

40 Ibid

41 ibid

42 ibid

43 "NARHA Presents Sis Gould Driving Recognition Award," *The Journal*, January 5, 2000

44 Debbie Gadus, "Working with Persons with Disabilities," presentation, April 2017

45 Cami Blanchard, "College Offers Major in Therapeutic Horsemanship," Lake Erie College Spring 2017 News

46 2017 *Annual Report*, Fieldstone Farm Therapeutic Riding Center

47 2016 *Annual Report*, Fieldstone Farm Therapeutic Riding Center